SECRET KEEPERS

2018
YOUNG WRITERS
SHORT FICTION CONTEST
WINNERS ANTHOLOGY

SECRET KEEPERS
The 2018 Young Writers Short Fiction Contest Winners Anthology
Copyright 2018 Wordcrafters in Eugene.

All Rights Reserved. This book may not be duplicated in any way—mechanical, photographic, electronic, or by means yet to be devised—without the written permission of the publisher, except in the case of brief excerpts or quotations for the purpose of review.

Wordcrafters in Eugene
438 Charnelton, Suite 102
Eugene, OR 97401

www.wordcraftersineugene.org

Wordcrafters in Eugene

Staff

Daryll Lynne Evans, Executive Director

Jorah LaFleur, WITS Coordinator

Drea Lee, Program Coordinator

Leah Velez, Program Coordinator

Zoe Herron, Intern

Board of Directors

Patricia Marshall, President

Christina Lay

Matt Lowes

Juanita Metzler

Wendy Morgan

Anthology Staff

Editors: Daryll Lynne Evans, Drea Lee, Leah Velez, and Zoe Herron

Design: Luminare Press

Writers in the Schools

Writers-in-Residence

Carter McKenzie
Jorah LaFleur

Visiting Authors

Myrlin Hepworth
Melissa Hart

Participating Schools

Creswell High School
Kalapuya High School
Phoenix Program at John Serbu Youth Campus
Willamette High School

Writers in the Schools is a program of Wordcrafters in Eugene, a non-profit literary arts organization whose mission is to provide writers and readers opportunities to strengthen their craft, deepen their connection with literature, and share their knowledge with each other and with future generations. For more information please contact:

Wordcrafters in Eugene
438 Charnelton, Suite 102
Eugene, OR 97401
www.wordcraftersineugene.org

Sponsors

Eugene Metro Rotary

Oregon Country Fair

Elizabeth George Foundation

Cow Creek Umpqua Indian Foundation

Herbert A. Templeton Foundation

Mills Davis Foundation

Pacific Continental Bank

Autzen Foundation

Harvest Foundation

Juan Young Trust

Braemer Charitable Trust

Café Yumm

Luminare Press

Individual Donors

Stacy Allen
Mark Brauner
Terry Brooks
Bill Cameron
Al and Liz Cratty
Kay Crider
Anne Dean
Vicki Elmer
Daryll Lynne Evans
Patricia Marshall
Sarah Finlay
Val Ford
Elizabeth George
Lynda Green
Louann Guzman
Tracy Habecker
Michael Harris

Kim Hunter
Kali Kardas
Elise Kimmons
Stephanie LeMenager
Matt Lowes
M.K. Martin
Juanita Metzler
Rex Moody
Kevin O'Brien
Svetlana Osadchuk
Susan Palmer
Susan Ploeger
Ellen Saunders
Morgan Songi
Janet Steward
Tex Thompson

Contents

WORDCRAFTERS IN EUGENE III
WRITERS IN THE SCHOOLS V
SPONSORS VI
INDIVIDUAL DONORS VII
INTRODUCTION 1
FICTION CONTEST WINNERS 4

ON THE CASE

MR. PIG AND THE MISSING PIE 7
   Naomi Delf
R.E.S.C.U.E 11
   Hannah J. Ellingsworth
GOOD OLD MRS. ROBINWAY 21
   Serena Jones

FUTURE SO BRIGHT

MY SISTER THE LAWBREAKER 29
   Kiri Sinha
ARCHAEA 39
   Sydney Crews
MY SUPERPOWER 43
   Lexis Sixel

FLIGHTS AND FIGHTS

The Journey to Devotion 49
    Anna Masonic
When a Meerkat Seeks the Snow 57
    Ella Schmeling
Happy Daze 68
    Clayton Su-Parker
Socks' Rebellion 78
    Ellie Urbancic

TRUTH IS STRANGER THAN FICTION

The Botanist 82
    Emily Krauss
Cliffhanger 86
    McKenna Hein
The Witch of Warrensville 90
    Sander Moffitt

Introduction

Dear Readers,

Has five years flown by already?! As Wordcrafters in Eugene celebrates its fifth year, we marvel at how far we've come since that first writing conference, which featured poetry workshops for youth and our very first Young Writers Short Fiction Contest, with forty entries from eager young writers looking for an outlet to share their work.

In our fifth year of the contest in 2018, almost 200 entries poured in from across Lane County, teachers loved the engaging curriculum we developed to help bring creative writing to their classrooms, and—thanks to Luminare Press— young writers get to see their words in print in the new Winners Anthology!

Five years ago, we began with a mission: *Wordcrafters provides writers and readers opportunities to strengthen their craft, deepen their connection with literature, and share their knowledge with each other and with future generations.*

Wordcrafters in Eugene has built a strong foundation for our Writers in the Schools (WITS) program. Since its launch, the WITS program has served over 4100 students in six school districts, including schools in rural and under-served areas.

In 2017-2018 WITS writing residencies focused on the message "Your Voice Matters." All WITS programs strive to give young writers a space to tell their stories. Our goal is to empower students to find their voice and understand their voice is powerful. Writing is, of course, important, but that is only the first step.

What we see time and again in our WITS program is how important it is to create a space for young writers to share their stories with each other and with the world. Whether it's reading their work aloud in a school or seeing their words in print, when students have the opportunity to hear others respond to their writing, to have others read their work, they finally understand the power of their voice and their stories.

Most notably for the 2017-2018 school year, we held six writer residencies: three in Kalapuya High School, and three in the Phoenix Program at John Serbu Youth Campus. WITS Writers Residency Series places professional writers in Lane County classrooms. These residencies give students the opportunity to work alongside a professional writer over the course of eight to ten weeks as part of their school day.

Students get to explore creative writing with a focus on the whole writing process, from composition through drafting, revising, polishing, and finally public performance and publication. We believe creative writing instruction creates a bridge to stronger writing and stronger academic performance across the curriculum. Studying alongside a professional writer gives students the opportunity to see what professional writing looks like up close. It also helps students to find their voice and empowers them to tell their stories.

Our Writers-in-Residence for 2017-2018 were activist and poet Carter McKenzie, and spoken word poet (and our new WITS Coordinator) Jorah LaFleur.

Each fall, we bring nationally-recognized spoken word poet and teaching artist Myrlin Hepworth to rural schools for spoken word poetry performances and writing workshops. This winter, WITS held the first annual Out Loud Poetry Slam.

We hope you enjoy this year's Winners Anthology, featuring thirteen talented writers. We love these stories of solving tricky mysteries, persevering in the face of defeat, standing up for what's right, and a lot of secrets!

This anthology illustrates that no matter where you have been or where you are going, the power of your voice is valuable tool for inspiration and vision. The participants of WITS reveal in their writing a capacity for imagination, vulnerability, and possibility that deserves to be heard. Read on!

Sincerely,

Daryll Lynne Evans, Executive Director,
Wordcrafters in Eugene

2018 Young Writers Short Fiction Contest Winners

Elementary School Division

1st: Naomi Delf, "Mr. Pig and the Missing Pie"
  Adams Elementary School
2nd: Hannah J. Ellingsworth, "R.E.S.C.U.E"
  Willagillespie Elementary School
3rd: Anna Masonic, "The Journey to Devotion"
  Twin Oaks Elementary
Honorable Mention: Emily Krauss, "The Botanist"
  Pleasant Hill Elementary

Middle School Division

1st: Kiri Sinha, "My Sister the Lawbreaker"
  Roosevelt Middle School
2nd: Clayton Su-Parker, "Happy Daze"
  Arts and Technology Academy
3rd: Ella Schmeling, "When a Meerkat Seeks the Snow"
  Monroe Middle School
Honorable Mention: Ellie Urbancic, "Socks' Rebellion"
  Roosevelt Middle School

High School Division

1st: Sander Moffitt, "The Witch of Warrensville"
    South Eugene High School
2nd: Serena Jones, "Good Old Mrs. Robinway"
    Baker Academy
2nd: Lexis Sixel, "My Superpower"
    Sheldon High School
3rd: McKenna Hein, "Cliffhanger"
    South Eugene High School
Honorable Mention: Sydney Crews "Archaea"
    South Eugene High School

ON THE CASE

Mr. Pig and the Missing Pie

Naomi Delf

Adams Elementary School

PART 1: MR. PIG

Mr. Pig was the best neighbor you could ask for. That was because he was a baker, so he was always making sweets for his friends.

One day, just as Mr. Pig was getting ready to close up his bakery, one of his best friends, Sir Turtle, came running into the bakery. Well, running as fast as an ancient turtle can run, which really isn't very fast. He was very out of breath.

As Sir Turtle stood panting in the doorway, Mr. Pig quickly got down from the ladder he was standing on to wash the window.

"What happened?" he asked.

"The Pie! It's gone!" Sir Turtle said. Then his arms, legs, tail, and head popped into his shell.

PART 2: THE CASE

After quite a bit of persuasion, Mr. Pig finally got Sir Turtle to come out of his shell and tell him more. They were sitting at one of the bakery tables.

"Sir Turtle, I can't help you if you don't tell me what's wrong!" Mr. Pig said. Sir Turtle took a deep breath and spoke.

"The famous statue of the Crown Pie has been stolen. Detective Hopper has asked me to solve the case!" Sir Turtle said excitedly.

"B-but what if I can't figure it out? What if the thief gets away, and everyone hates me and, and…." And then, Sir Turtle broke into tears. He was a very emotional man.

PART 3: THE SCENE

Mr. Pig helped Sir Turtle put on his jacket. After a quick cup of tea to calm Sir Turtle's nerves, the two walked out the door, and headed down the road to the scene of the crime.

When they arrived at the crime scene, young Mr. Chipper the chipmunk rushed to ask them a bunch of questions.

"Do you know who it is? Any prime suspects?" Mr. Chipper asked excitedly.

"Relax! We haven't even seen the crime scene yet!" said Mr. Pig. As they drew closer to the place of the missing pie, Mr. Pig gasped.

"What?" Sir Turtle asked.

"It's gone! I mean, totally gone! All of it!" he exclaimed.

"Well, yes. It is a *missing pie*, isn't it?" Sir Turtle said.

Sir Turtle and Mr. Pig soon arrived at the place where the sculpture once stood.

PART 4: CLUES

Sir Turtle was great at solving cases, but even he was stumped on this one.

"Yelp!" Mr. Pig said.

"What?" Sir Turtle asked.

"I found something!" he replied.

Sir Turtle rushed to see what he found. Mr. Pig was inspecting something at the base of a nearby tree. There was a small patch of thick, white, creamy stuff.

"What's that?" Sir Turtle asked, already knowing the answer.

"It's frosting," said Mr. Pig.

PART 5: SUSPECTS

Sir Turtle and Mr. Pig had rushed home to think about the case.

"Who are the suspects?" Mr. Pig asked Sir Turtle for the millionth time.

"Everyone," he moaned, "Or at least everyone who likes food with frosting, which is everyone."

"Actually, not everyone…." Mr. Pig stopped. Sir Turtle was glaring at him.

"Anyway, how are we going to catch this guy? Or gal, I guess," Mr. Pig asked.

"I don't know," Sir Turtle said. Sir Turtle stood up and walked home.

Mr. Pig yawned. Slowly, he walked home and went to bed.

When Sir Turtle woke up in the morning, he gasped.

"I know who it is!" he exclaimed to himself. He rushed out the door.

Mr. Pig was ready when Sir Turtle burst into the bakery.

"It was Dr. Raccoon!" They said at the exact same time.

Dr. Raccoon was a raccoon with a talent for theft. He worked at a doctor's office. There was a little sweet shop in the waiting room for patients. Everyone knew that Dr. Raccoon took things from the little shop, but no one really cared. He must have had some frosting left on his hands from a cupcake when he stole the Crown Pie.

PART 6: THE ARREST

For over a week, Mr. Pig and Sir Turtle watched Dr. Raccoon. They would put on disguises and wait in the waiting room of the doctor's office he worked in. Mr. Pig even went so far as to rent out a mail delivery van and park it in front of Dr. Raccoon's house so he could see him. But still, nothing. Dr. Raccoon showed almost no signs of stealing the pie. The only thing suspicious was that he ate a lot of pie. But they assumed that was normal.

At the bakery, Mr. Pig and Sir Turtle sat at a table, thinking. Slowly, Sir Turtle sighed.

"I had hoped I wouldn't have to do this. We might just have to check the surveillance cameras," Sir Turtle said.

"There was video footage?!" Mr. Pig yelled, "I wasted a whole week in a van when there was video footage?!"

"Well, yes," Sir Turtle said.

"Would you like to go watch it now?" he asked, exasperated. Grumpily, Mr. Pig walked to the police station with Sir Turtle. After watching the footage, they determined it was, in fact, Dr. Raccoon who stole the pie. After the arrest, Mr. Pig and Sir Turtle once again sat at the bakery table.

"I'm still mad at you," Mr. Pig said.

"I know," Sir Turtle replied with a slight smile. He chuckled his old turtle laugh. Mr. Pig chuckled too.

"Friends?" Sir Turtle asked.

"Friends," Mr. Pig said.

And that was that.

R.E.S.C.U.E

Hannah J. Ellingsworth
Willagillespie Elementary School

My name is Baxter Gingernoodle. I'm a Yorkshire Terrier, and people call me tiny. Granted, I am tiny, but I do more than some people would think. My owner is Chloe. She is ten years old, which I learned at school. Dogs don't go to school, right? Wrong.

I learned that most dogs only speak "dog," a language that humans use to describe the way dogs speak to each other. But I understand several ways humans speak. That's why I got accepted into SDSC. That stands for the Smart Dogs Spy College. Key word: spy.

This morning I got a text from my boss, General Carly.

Carly: Code red!
Baxter: What is the emergency?
Carly: SOS! The Operation is coming!
Baxter: Got it. I'm coming right now!

The Operation is our rival spy team. It's made of all cats and operated by General Snowball. She is a dangerously cute cat. All that white fluff is covering the evil in her heart. I ran downstairs. "BARK BARK BARK BARK!"

"Baxter! What do you want? I just finished doing chores and I want to sit down!" whined Chloe.

"Chloe! I have to get to the school now! It's an emergency!"

Of course, all she heard was *BARK BARK BARK*!

"All right! You win!" she said.

I dashed outside. As I entered my giant dog house, my blue hologram keypad popped up. I punched in my code, 656971770. My dog house buzzed as the yellow walls faded to dirt. I fell way down the long tunnel into the main room of the spy lab. I opened my eyes to the bustle of all the busy dogs preparing for the arrival of The Operation.

"Hi Baxter! I can't believe you finally made it!" said my friend, Sadie.

So we waited. Hours and hours later, still nothing came.

"I can't believe they didn't show up!" I exclaimed.

It was absurd. The only thing that came was pounding rain.

Later, we got a report from the UCI. That stands for the Undercover Canine Investigation. It's like an undercover dog police team that streams throughout five states. We have schools set up in Nevada, California, Idaho, Oregon, and Washington.

The report was about a string of robberies in Carson City, Nevada. The robberies were about missing supplies in pet stores. I was thinking, who in their right mind would want to rob a pet store? Oh!

"It's obvious that The Operation did it."

"That's it! We have proof!" exclaimed Sadie.

"It's not that simple though. The Operation is an experienced team. They wouldn't do something like this unless they did it on purpose. I know Snowball and her crew have a plan. She's smart, but we're smarter!" But, then it hit me. "We have to stop them! Ally lives near there!"

Ally was a cat my family used to have. We did everything together. Then, we found out that Mom was allergic to cats. We had to give Ally to our friends, the Robinsons. I can't imagine what would happen if she became part of The Operation. What if Ally was...evil? We had to save her!

"Baxter, we have business to take care of. We're very busy holding back The Operation. I don't have time for you to chat on the phone," Carly told me.

"Aw, come on! I need to make a call for The Office. I know someone who might be a victim of The Operation! She is a cat I know, who—" I didn't finish.

"Oh, no way! If she is a cat, I am not going to help her."

I decided I had to take drastic measures. My plan was to sneak out of the school early so that I could go warn Ally before it was too late. "It may or may not work. Wish me good luck!"

Anyway, it was currently 8:39 p.m., and I was ready to go into action. I casually strolled over towards the big red doors blocking the entrance. I gave them a hard tug. Locked. I glanced around the hallway. I knew this place like the back of my paw.

I quickly and silently unlatched the silver door of the nearest fire escape. Next, I slowly dragged the door open. I felt the gust of night wind outside. There are six floors of the school. Most of which are underground. The only way to get in or out is to go through the sixth floor, because it is the only one that is above ground.

I stepped out and let the door slip shut behind me. The cool autumn breeze blew my fur in every direction. Then I looked down at the beautiful meadows below me with the red leaves and the green grass.

I let out a whimper and jumped back, suddenly realizing I was leaning over the edge of the railing. I silenced myself, for fear I was going to get caught. Almost as if my vision had come to life, I heard a voice. I saw a shadow darting across the field in front of me. I recognized the voice I had heard so many times before. It was Ally!

"Who's there? Never sneak up on me!"

A bright light was shined directly at my face, momentarily blinding me. "Ally! It's me! Baxter?"

I could tell she couldn't find me. "I'm up here! I was about to go and save you but I don't remember how to get down!"

"Well, my hero!" Ally rolled her eyes.

She is, what she calls, a strong girl-power enthusiast. Ally believes that girls shouldn't have to be rescued by boys. That they can do things themselves. I do like her in that way, because she never judges me for being best friends with a girl like some of the other dogs do.

She also believes that cats have different mindsets than dogs. By that, I mean that she thinks cats are smarter. When she says that, I always ask her, do cats have their own spy programs in five different states? Oh no. I forgot about The Operation.

Since Ally's already here, I can protect her from The Operation.

"Why are you here, anyway, Ally?"

The question echoed through the air, but was never answered. It was just then that I realized the flashlight had been shut off. The space around me was as pitch black as it was before. And I hadn't heard Ally's voice in a while, actually. Then it hit me...she was gone.

I started my slow descent down the ladder of the fire escape. The air was seemingly colder than before. Oh no! I almost slid off the ladder when I remembered something very important. It was currently 10:26 p.m., almost two hours later than when I left at 8:39! What if my owners found out about my career as a spy?

I get to leave school at 9:00. My owner, Chloe, gets home

at 9:30. That gives me just enough time to pretend I've been home all day. I eat all my dog food, scatter some toys on the floor, and chew on some furniture. Chloe finds me at home, lying on our family's tan couch, and snuggling up to my favorite blanket. So, what would happen when she got home and couldn't find me anywhere? I was going to have a lot of explaining to do.

As these thoughts swam through my head, I quickened my speed down the ladder. As fast as I could go without falling, I made it down. About six rungs from the ground, I braced myself, and jumped. As soon as my paws hit the ground, I dashed down the path that led home. For a moment, time seemed to go in slow motion. I ran and jumped over fallen tree branches.

Finally, panting and exhausted, I returned to my house. Somehow, I'm going to have to tell Chloe about SDSC. Obviously, I can't talk. But there is this one thing that I can do.

Completely prepared, I marched in through my doggy door.

"I'm home!"

No one was there. I tried Chloe's room instead. She was sitting on her bed, reading *Wonder*. I whimpered softly, and she looked up.

"Baxter! Where have you been? I missed you so much!"

I whimpered. Not because I was sad, but because it was time. Time to spill out all of my secrets to Chloe. I pawed at her computer. She quickly got the message and opened it up. Next came the hardest part.

I needed Chloe to open the notepad app. I know! I went over to her bookshelf and dragged out at drawing pad. At first, she was confused. Then I saw that "now I get it" look on her face. She clicked on the app and I shoved my way onto her lap.

Chloe watched in awe as I begun to type. I typed out all of my spy info, including the fact that I know how to type. Pretty cool right? Do you really think a human could be this creative? Anyway, now that Chloe knew everything, she could help me rescue Ally!

Things did not go how I expected. Chloe seemed to think that something horrid was going to happen, that the world would somehow end.

"Baxter! We have to save Ally! They have her all tied up, I know it! Is the world going to end, Baxter? Is it? Please tell me you know!" she exclaimed.

I could tell Chloe was close to tears by now. I really wanted to crawl up in her lap, to tell her that everything was going to be okay. I wanted to tell her that I knew how to fix everything. But I couldn't. Because I didn't.

"I can't, Chloe! Okay? I know you count on me to help you, to always be there for you. But sometimes it just doesn't work like that! I don't know everything and neither does anyone else." I didn't want to, but I typed out all of those words I said in "Dog."

At that moment, Chloe burst into tears. I felt so bad. I just didn't think I was ready for a mission like this. What if they hurt me? What if they hurt my family and my friends?

But then, Chloe stopped crying. She looked me right in the eye and said, "Baxter! I know you are so scared. Believe me, I know. Remember the time that we went bungee jumping? I was so scared. But I did it, and I had fun! Spying is your bridge! Once you jump, you aren't going to fall. You are going to fly! You can change the world. You are a really brave dog. You are a hero! And heroes don't change the world when they're sitting on my bed!"

Chloe's little speech was empowering. I was going to

conquer those stupid cats. And when I did, I knew at least Chloe will be proud of me. She was the most loyal sister ever.

"Don't be scared, Baxter. I'm not supposed to tell you this, but you have something special that no one else has. A secret power, maybe?"

I wondered what she meant by secret power? Well, I always said R.E.S.C.U.E. was my favorite acronym; Ready, Energy, Save, Create, Unstoppable, and Elaborate. I was going to Take. Them. Down!

I nuzzled Chloe as a goodbye. After that, I climbed up on the bed and stared out the window. Perfect. Then, I hurtled out the window, imaginary cape soaring behind me, and silently landed on my feet.

I saw the look of anguish on Chloe's face as she poked her head out the window to watch. I turned around and winked.

"Couldn't you have taken the door?!"

But I didn't hear her, because I was already running down the pavement to my fate.

"What is the puny mutt doing here?"

It was The Operation's security guard, Butch. This was perfect.

"Oh, Butch. You know what I'm here for."

At first, he looked confused.

"Oh, right. The little cat. Boss wanted to talk to you about that," he said.

"I bet you didn't figure I was going to do this!" I grabbed his paw and flipped him over. He hit the ground with a thud. So easy.

I dashed through the entrance to the building. But, I just walked down the halls, attacking everything that got in my way. I started to hear a strange noise. It was a very loud buzzing.

I followed the noise until I came to a room labeled "Large Buzzing Generator." I thought that must be some kind of code name. I heard a noise that sounded like fighting, too. That was it. It was time. I kicked the door open!

Everything paused.

"Ally?!"

"Baxter?!"

Snowball from The Operation was in there, too. Before me stood a giant, silver tank. I think Snowball saw me staring.

"It's a 2,000-pound giant electromagnetic generator. It powers the entire building," she said, smugly.

"Wait, why are you here, Baxter?" asked Ally.

"I came to rescue you! But, I guess you didn't need it," I replied.

"I don't need someone to come help me. I have this under control!" She didn't sound like she meant it.

"Oh. Well I—." Suddenly, I was being lifted off the ground. "What are you doing?!"

"Throwing you in the pit!" cackled Snowball. She let out an evil, witchlike laugh.

It was then I noticed that there was an opening at the top of the generator. They were going to throw me in it! I also realized it wasn't a generator at all, it was a pit for their victims!

I let out a scream as they climbed the stairs to the top. What was I going to do? There was nothing I could do. These cats were bigger than me, and stronger.

There was one thing I could do.

"Ally, you will always be my sister!" And they tossed me in the pit. I clung to the edge of the big, metal cave. Dove was lifting my claws from it, one by one. Below me, there was a vast sea of green, toxic liquid.

Dove and Snowball both grinned as they lifted the last

claw from the edge. Then, I fell fifteen feet down to the toxic water of the pit. Ally shrieked, and then I was submerged.

I doggy paddled my way to the surface. I tried to avoid drinking the liquid for fear that it was poisonous. I had to find a way out. This would not be Baxter Gingernoodle's last day! I was going to return from this mission to Chloe, who loved me. I gathered up all of my courage, and I swam to the bottom of the pit.

I knew it! There was a hole at the bottom. Just big enough to drain the pit. And, big enough for a tiny dog! I tried as hard as I could to swim into the drain hole. It sucked me up and led me down the tunnel. I rode the current like a waterslide all the way down.

Eventually, I stood up, and I marched down to Ally again. Once again, I kicked the door open.

"I, Baxter Gingernoodle, will not be defeated!"

I was met with stares of awe.

"Baxter, you're alive!" exclaimed Ally with joy.

Snowball got right to the point. "Invincible, eh? Maybe we should defeat her instead!" She grinned, pointing at Ally.

"No, you won't!" I screamed, infuriated.

Suddenly, they were hit by a force of electricity that not even Snowball was capable of. Where did it come from? I gasped. It came from me! My paws were crackling with blue sparks.

"Baxter, what is going on?" Ally questioned.

"What is happening to me?!" I shrieked, then I collapsed onto the floor.

Everything went black.

Next thing I knew, I was lying on Chloe's bedroom floor. Ally was there, too.

"He's waking up!" alerted Ally.

"What's going on? What happened?" I asked, groggily.

"You electrocuted the cats, and then you passed out," Ally said. "I found Chloe and she took you home," she informed me.

"Where are the cats?" I asked, finally.

"They were found and taken to the shelter. All of The Operation was, actually."

Then, I realized that Chloe couldn't understand me talking to Ally. She handed me the laptop and I told her everything that happened to me.

"So that is the secret power that you told me about!" I typed.

"Yes. I really wanted to tell you, but I was instructed by your previous owner not to. I didn't know how to activate it anyway, she wouldn't tell me. It must have been a chemical in the toxic liquid!" Chloe replied.

Now everything made sense. I had superpowers! That was awesome! I could now do everything I had always wanted to do!

"It's pretty cool. But, training on how to use them starts tomorrow," Chloe told me.

"Aw, man!" I typed. Then we all laughed.

The next day, I was promoted to General of The Office. I was the leader, head spy! A month after that, my story was in the paper, and later, made into a movie! Chloe got a ton of money and spent it all on me!

In two years we got a puppy! His name was Gizmo, and I taught him how to be a spy. Once I was old, I couldn't be a spy anymore, and Gizmo took my place as General. I spent the rest of my life making inventions for The Office. Me and Chloe were famous, life was great, and I loved it like that.

Good Old Mrs. Robinway

Serena Jones

Baker Academy

In the busy city of Harper, Kansas, there was a simple office. It was a little building that nestled between the museum and the antique store on Dodd Street since before anyone could really recall. The funny thing was, no one really knew what the office did. The manager of the building, Mr. Grey, wasn't much help.

"We file taxes," he would reply to the ever-curious Girl Scout.

"Life insurance," he would tell the nosy Mrs. Turnpike.

"Printing," he would say quickly to the museum owner trying to make small talk.

Of course, it wasn't any of those things. The city folk were clueless. They believed it was the best tax/insurance/printing office they had ever seen. Mr. Grey's job was to make sure that it stayed that way.

Because, in reality, the office was a disguised safe house for international spies. Every member was sent all over the world, foiling terrorists' plans one day and stopping wars the next. Mr. Grey had created the office as a place that spies could relax in anonymity.

Most spies were very young. Forty-two-year old Mr. Grey was the oldest by far. The life of a spy was dangerous after all. There was only one person who was older, and she had been at the office before anyone else. The elite, ever mysterious widow, Mrs. Robinway. Tomorrow would be her sixty-third birthday.

Mrs. Robinway didn't look like much more than an old lady, with powder-white hair and wrinkles around her eyes and mouth. Every time she smiled they would crease. Whenever she held something, her mild arthritis would make her hands quiver. Still, she had gained the respect of every spy at the office.

She seemed to always hold up her cover as an office secretary who sorted mail and greeted visitors. The newer recruits, aged from twelve to twenty, liked her for her cover's approachability. They could always count on her to have a jar of candies in seasonal colors sitting invitingly on her desk for everyone. The only problem with the supposed "elite" was one tiny detail: unbeknownst to the spies, she wasn't actually a spy.

She believed they were actually at a printing office. She had come to the office a decade ago, wanting something to get her mind off her deceased husband. Mr. Grey had happily welcomed her, believing that she, too, had heard the news that spies were welcome. She spent her days filing paperwork, which was actually spies sending messages back and forth in code. Her clueless attitude seemed, to the other spies at least, to be her expert acting.

* * *

"Mrs. Robinway!" Mr. Grey barked.

Mrs. Robinway looked away from the cat poster she was tacking up.

"How can I help you, Wallis?" she asked kindly.

The manager's breath caught in his throat for moment and he had to cough. Mrs. Robinway had a way of using her mystique to catch him off guard. He cleared his throat and straightened up.

"Mr. Grey," he grunted. "Mrs. Robinway, let's try to

keep it professional. Now, do you still have that file I asked to keep safe?"

He gave her a knowing look that Mrs. Robinway didn't bother to acknowledge. To her, Mr. Grey was an overly dramatic boss. How important could a couple files for a printing office be?

She spun around in her chair, thumbed through her filing cabinet, and pulled out a bright red folder. She handed it to him and for a split second, their fingers touched.

Mr. Grey gave her a shy smile, which was uncharacteristic for him. Mrs. Robinway smiled too, albeit slightly confused. What a strange man.

After a minute, he regained his serious disposition and cleared his throat yet again.

"Ahem, ahem! Thank you, for the file. I believe two of our younger interns wished to speak to you before going on their mission," he said quickly, then darted into his office.

Mrs. Robinway smiled. She knew who the interns would be. Keith and Lynn. She loved them much like she loved her own grandchildren. They were lovely boys. Sure enough, the two young men approached her desk, looking rather stressed.

Lynn, the fun-loving redhead, reached into her candy jar to pull out a handful of red, orange, and yellow M&Ms. Keith, the more pessimistic one, gave him a disapproving look as Lynn shoved all the candies into his mouth at the same time.

"'Ello, Mrs. Robinway, we're off to the, uh, 'copy supply store,'" Lynn said, his voice muffled by the ridiculous amount of sweets in his mouth.

Lynn was a new recruit, and wasn't very good with his cover. He also hadn't quite trained away his evident Irish accent, which some spies liked to tease him about. He was a good kid, though, through and through. Keith was admittedly a bit of a brat at times, but he watched out for Lynn. Keith wouldn't admit it, but he cared a lot about him.

Keith gave him another look of disdain.

"Uh, and we were, uh, wonderin' if you could give us a bit of advice or anythin' to help us out. You being the elite here and all," he offered, anxiously twisting his hands.

Keith rolled his eyes. He often doubted Mrs. Robinway. In fact, he didn't think she was a real spy. Lynn firmly disagreed and was always trying to prove him wrong.

Mrs. Robinway smiled.

"Oh, ho, ho. Well, I wouldn't call myself an elite, but I actually do happen to have something. You two are such good boys, and it's cold outside. I made you these."

She fished under her desk and pulled out two hand-knit hats, blue for Lynn and black for Keith. Lynn took the hat and his face fell for a moment. Keith scoffed. He went to give Lynn a smug I-told-you-so look, but was surprised when Lynn jammed the black hat on his head and gave Mrs. Robinway a winning grin.

Lynn wasn't about to let his spirits get crushed so quickly. He just knew Mrs. Robinway was special.

"Thank you, Mrs. Robinway," he said quickly, and ushered Keith out the door before he could protest.

She smiled, the corners of her mouth crinkling like tissue paper. Those two boys always brightened her day.

* * *

The boys didn't return to the office for three days. Mrs. Robinway had to admit, she was a little worried. They were practically her adopted grandchildren, those boys. On the fourth day, however, they came bursting through the door with manic grins and bright eyes. Their hats were gone and their hair looked staticky.

"Goodness me, boys, where have you been?" Mrs. Robinway inquired.

Lynn gave her an ear-splitting smile. Keith looked somewhat reluctantly happy.

"Oh, Mrs. Robinway, we can't thank you enough for your wisdom! You are truly an elite to be praised!" he shouted.

Mrs. Robinway, unsure of the situation, blushed. "Oh, I'm just a dotty old lady, boys. What are you talking about?"

The boys smiled at each other. Mrs. Robinway was messing with them again. They rushed to tell their friends the good news.

A huge group of spies gathered anxiously, gasping at every frightening moment as Lynn spun their tale.

"And so there we were, cornered by at least a dozen, no, two dozen, of Doctor Blade's bots, absolutely no way out in sight."

An older recruit gasped. Everyone knew about Erica, who had lost her eye to one of those vile machines.

Lynn spread his arms wide dramatically, loving the attention he was getting. "And so this guy over here thought we were goners! That Mrs. Robinway wasn't a truly mighty spy!" he accused, playfully ruffling Keith's hair.

Keith rolled his eyes, but everyone could see he was smiling.

"And I said, 'Wait, the hats!', and we snatched them off our heads. True, the hats had given us away in the first place, but we didn't account for the old lady's brilliance! Without a moment to lose, the bots closing in with their pincers at our necks—"

Lynn jumped on a table, pantomiming a claw grappling for his neck. All the spies watched him with a mix of shock and amusement. Keith took a cautious step forward, just in case Lynn took an accidental dive.

"—and Keith whips out his lighter and we lit the hats!" His audience was silent.

"Ah, don't give up on me now! I'm just getting to the best part! It turns out wool is so flammable, it caused smoke to go up to the detectors! Every mad scientist has to have a good emergency system, right?"

Lynn grinned more and more as he saw pride reflected in his colleagues' eyes. Even the eldest were giving nods of approval.

"And sure enough, BAM! The sprinklers go off, short circuiting every bot within a half a mile radius! All of Doctor Blade's work went down the drain! You should've seen the man's face!"

A small girl with big freckles pushed her way to the front. She waved her hands until she got Lynn and Keith's attention.

"So did you get him? Is Doctor Blade finally in jail?"

Lynn took a deep inhale.

"Yes, he finally is, Jane! And it's all thanks to Mrs. Robinway!" he screamed happily, diving backwards off the table. Keith stumbled forward and just barely managed to catch him.

"Three cheers for Mrs. Robinway!" he yelled from Keith's arms.

The group of spies joined in to shout, "ROBINWAY, ROBINWAY, ROBINWAY!"

* * *

From upstairs, Mrs. Robinway chuckled, beside herself. Mr. Grey smirked at the muffled sounds of cheering.

"You've done a great deed for this office, Mrs. Robinway,"

he said proudly, crossing his arms.

She went red, her head down as she shuffled papers together.

"Oh, I didn't realize hats were such a big deal in this town. I suppose I'll have to make more," she giggled.

Mr. Grey cocked his head slightly in confusion, then realized she was just pulling his leg. Trust her to be so modest.

"I'm serious, Mrs. Robinway, I don't know what we would do without your assistance to this fine facility."

She took a deep breath.

"Probably fall apart, I suppose," she said, snorting.

Mr. Grey felt his heart flutter at her simple laugh. Truly, Mrs. Robinway was a spy to be respected.

"Seriously, Mrs. Robinway, we must celebrate. You've just saved two of our men."

From certain frostbite, I suppose, she thought to herself. What else could Mr. Grey have meant?

"Oh, no, Mr. Grey. Celebrating sounds lovely, but I have several papers I promised to have on your desk. By the way, when did you want those? Monday or Tuesday?" she asked with one of her honey-sweet smiles.

Mr. Grey smiled wryly back. A single tear welled up in his eye. Mrs. Robinway, a true saint. Dedicated to her cover no matter what. She was right. They would fall apart without her guidance and expertise.

"Mr. Grey?"

Mr. Grey sniffled, that tear sliding down his cheek.

"Good old Mrs. Robinway," he said, brushing the tear away with a stroke of his fist.

Mrs. Robinway stared at him, slightly concerned as he continued to cry.

"I'll just get them in on Monday, then."

FUTURE SO BRIGHT

My Sister the Lawbreaker

Kiri Sinha

Roosevelt Middle School

Four. Four is the number of people who know my secret. It was two, before Lark found out. Before Lark told Blythe.

Blythe approaches me. She is wearing a blood red coat. She smells of a mix of burning wood and crushed flowers.

"Skai, please sit," she says.

I oblige, pulling out a plastic yellow seat from under the large desk.

Lark enters the room, pushing open the heavy oak door as silently as possible. He pulls out his own yellow chair and avoids looking me in the eye.

Blythe is our Gaya. Except she's his Birther too. Which is illegal. His secret that I never told.

"Skai, a few days ago, you were caught by Lark participating in an unacceptable act," says Blythe. "By unacceptable, I mean illegal."

"I know," I reply, briefly glancing at the ceiling, "but you should know better than anyone the importance of family."

Real family. It's a threat. I thought through my blows carefully. Blythe is not allowed to have Lark. He should be with another Gaya, across the Earth. She knows that.

"That does not concern your actions," she replies.

She seems a bit taken aback, though it's not completely unexpected of me to say something like this.

"I think it does." I don't want to waste any time getting to the point of this conversation. I want it to be done, so whenever I have an empty moment I can mull it over in my mind, thinking of what I should have said and should have done, and eventually those words will become a reality. In my mind, at least.

My confidence towards Blythe is faked. Secretly, I can't stand the lies. I remember a science experiment we did at school once. We took a tooth and dropped it into a bottle of Coke. The Coke slowly ate away at the tooth. Eventually, there was no tooth. There was only Coke. Right now, my heart is the tooth and my lies are the Coke.

"It was a simple mistake that placed you here, Skai. But it was your mistake to seek out your sister," says Blythe. Her eyes are clear and a tiny bit wet. They don't meet mine. They never have. I love Blythe. I mean, she's my Gaya, but you have to love your Gaya more than anyone else. At least you're supposed to, but I don't. Blythe cares for me, but she's really just that—a caretaker. A distant one, at best.

"It was not a mistake. I stand behind my actions. I deserve to know my own sister. I love her more than anyone here, and she's helped me more than you ever will." Blythe flinches at my words. Her hazel eyes glaze over for a moment, then return to their normal state. Lark has those same eyes. A lot of people have hazel eyes. I do. So does Raven, my sister. And the mailman. As does the woman who delivers our newspaper. I could go on. Eye color doesn't mean anything.

Slowly, people are beginning to look more and more alike. Every family house is a literal melting pot. Children from all over the world are put in one place, where they grow up together. It's a good idea, in theory.

"Skai, your points are valid, but I am not the person you should make them to. You know perfectly well that blood ties are illegal."

"As you do," I say, "but that never stopped you." Lark looks at his feet. I wish he didn't have to be here for this.

"Skai, I'm going to tell you this right now: you must stop."

I decide to take a different approach. "How do you even know she's my sister?"

Blythe purses her lips then sighs. "It's too much of a risk—"

"At least let us take a DNA test," I cut in. I feel myself losing the argument, and I see my sister being taken away from me. I know that we'll never be able to get a test. It's illegal. But I have to try. Just for the sake of trying.

"There's no legal way to obtain the test without revealing what you have already done," Blythe replies. The way she says the words, as if she's thought about them many times. She probably has, I reflect.

I switch to pouting. "There has to be a way."

Blythe sucks in her cheeks. "I have one. From my wedding." People are required to take the test before getting married, to assure you aren't marrying a relative. Still, the fact that Blythe has one shows a dark side to my Gaya that I didn't know she was capable of.

"Thank you!" I gasp, leaping out of my seat to awkwardly hug her. Blythe sighs. So does Lark.

"Just...try not to get too disappointed. And if you are sisters, promise me, promise me, Skai, that you will break off all contact with her."

I squeeze my eyes shut and count to ten. When I open them again, the look on my face is dead serious. "I promise."

* * *

Raven and I met on a Monday. I was just leaving my first period class, World History. My head was buzzing with facts of the War that shaped our society, and I was trying to grasp the immense number of lives lost. That was the start of our system today. It was the orphans who were sent off, sent to the very first Gayas. And slowly society realized that that was the right thing to do. Send children away at birth to Gayas across the Earth. I had found myself wishing that the war never happened, that the system never started. I thought that, maybe, the world could be a better place if children were allowed to stay with their Birthers. I wasn't sure back then. Now I am positive.

As I crammed papers into my large purple binder, I felt a tap on my shoulder. I turned around, expecting to see a friend from my next class. Instead, I came face to face with an unfamiliar tenth grader. Our school went from sixth through twelfth grade, but I tended to avoid anyone who wasn't in my own grade, seventh. Thinking about it a bit more, I realized I vaguely recognized the girl from the school halls. I had noticed her before, not because of her black hair, or her slightly turned down lips, or her hazel eyes, which were all much like my own, but because of the way she carried herself. She always walked alone, and acted like she had fallen from heaven itself, and was simply blessing the Earth with her presence. I admired her for it. I still do.

Now that I could see her up close, I realized she was drop-dead beautiful. Scarily beautiful. Unfairly beautiful.

"Hi," I said. I raised my eyebrows at her when I didn't get a response. She looked me up and down, as if evaluating my worth. Eventually, she finished scrutinizing me, and seeming satisfied with what she saw, she smiled and said, "Hello."

"Hi. Again." I added awkwardly,

"Are you Skai?"

"Yes."

"I think you're my sister."

* * *

I didn't believe Raven that day, but I agreed to get coffee (well, in my case, hot chocolate) with her after school. After all, what was the worst that could happen? I didn't think that she had any ill-intentioned plans for me.

We went to a small cafe together and we did my homework. Raven, it turned out, was one of those really smart people who you would be totally annoyed with, except they're also extremely helpful.

She was able to explain how to graph a $y = mx + b$ equation well enough that I was able to get an A on my next quiz. The Monday cafe meetup became a weekly ritual, as well as my newly improved math grades.

Raven never told me why she thought we were sisters. I asked her once, and she just shrugged it off. I didn't have a reason to believe we weren't sisters, though. We acted like sisters, or what I thought sisters should act like. I went to Raven whenever I needed help with anything. She would hear about my teachers, my friends, Lark, Blythe, my fish, my clothing, my swimming, and anything else that was on my mind. Then she would offer me advice, and I would think to myself again how grateful I was that she found me.

I like to think that I helped Raven, too. Before I even knew her, I realized that she was always alone. Something about her seemed to scare people away. Maybe it was because she was afraid of them. She rarely looked anyone in the eye or returned a simple hello.

Raven and I may not be blood relatives, but if this society has taught me anything, it's that she is definitely my sister. After all, what is a sister other than someone you spend time with who helps you?

* * *

Blythe gets up to answer a knock on the door. I already know who it is. Raven. I hear her voice, soft but clear.

"Hello."

"Hello," replies Blythe.

"Please come in."

I see my sister's tired face. She offers me a small smile, then loses it in the effort of sighing. Just as quickly as it went blank, her expression morphs as she sees Lark and realizes he revealed our secret. I'm not sure why Blythe insisted on him being here. Maybe it's because he is her birth son. I realize I am being unfair. It is more likely due to the fact that he is the one who found us out.

Raven places herself lightly on our leather couch. A barrier between me and Lark, still protecting me.

"Okay," says Blythe. "Now for the DNA test."

Before the War and the international decision to divide families, there was little demand for genetic tests. Now, they are used every day. Their main use is to avoid marrying blood relatives, but the government sometimes uses them otherwise. They are constantly being updated. Scientists and manufacturers have found a way to create them so they are accurate, quick to use, and cheap to produce. The government doesn't want people to know their blood families though, for fear of the people becoming divided again. This means that DNA tests are illegal to sell and use without a permit. The government tracks them closely, and there's a limit on the number you can use in a lifetime. Of course, this has created a black market for DNA tests. It's strange that Blythe has one; they're not easy to obtain.

Blythe stands in front of us. I look down at her boots. Blythe is usually miserly in her spending, but boots are the one thing she always splurges on.

"So... girls," she starts. She tries to avoid Raven's gaze, which is planted firmly on her, much as a snake would watch a mouse. She takes out the small box, which contains the test and flips it over to read the instructions. "Pull out a piece of your hair," she mumbles. "Make sure that it is pulled from your scalp; don't just break it off... et cetera, et cetera..."

I unwind my hair from its tight bun and let it fall over my shoulders in messy clumps. Raven reaches over and plucks a strand of it off my head. I frown at her playfully, and she half smirks. For the first time, I'm hit by the possibility that maybe Raven and I really are sisters. It seems so impossible, yet so real.

Raven holds the two strands of hair out in front of her, in a rare ray of sunlight. They sway in a nonexistent breeze. They are identical. The same lonely black color. Blythe takes them from Raven's hand. She is careful not to drop them. She is opening the box that contains the test when we hear a knock on the door. It is sharp and quick, one single rap. Blythe's face turns as pale as a cloud on a sunny day.

"In the name of the law, open your door!" A loud voice booms.

I feel my mind slide down my throat and slosh into my stomach. Blythe's feet seem glued to the ground, so Raven stands up instead. The old oak door lets out a groan. Two men smile nervously at us. They're dressed in black. Around their waists they have heavy belts weighted with objects I don't recognize.

Raven steps back nervously, forcing a tiny smile that doesn't fit on her solemn face. The men welcome themselves into our living room, grinding dirt into our white carpet with their heavy shoes. Their gazes shift from Blythe to Lark to Raven to me, and then to the test in Blythe's hand.

One of the men walks towards Blythe. He smiles. It's a sad but satisfied look, like a scientist watching the hurricane they predicted to happen appear on the radar.

"Would I be wrong to assume that that is a DNA test in your hand?" he asks Blythe. She bites her lip nervously, her eyes darting around the room. I hear Lark let out a forced breath of air beside me.

"No, sir. You would not be incorrect."

* * *

After that, there is not much we can do. There is no way Blythe can stay with us. They give her two hours to pack everything up, kiss Lark and me goodbye, and sob so much the skin on her cheeks turn raw. Lark cries too. His eyes turn red, and snot dribbles off his chin and onto his shorts. I am too scared to cry. Too shocked. I sit on the couch and don't move until it's time for Blythe to leave.

Raven sits next to me, her hand in mine, her features blank and wet with tears. The two men grab both of Blythe's wrists and are about to take her away, take her away forever, throw her in jail just because the government doesn't want people to be with their own families when she calls, "Wait!"

Blythe elbows the men away and rushes towards the three of us, her face cold and solemn.

"Listen very closely," she says.

No one moves. One of the men coughs impatiently by the door.

Then Blythe whispers very quietly, "Lark is my birth son, and Skai...you are my birth daughter. Raven is your sister. Raven is," she pauses long enough to hear Raven's startled gasp of realization, then continues. "You are all my children."

She meets my eyes for the first time. One tear falls from my face and onto my hand. It carries the weight of Blythe's words, of what just happened, and of what was about to happen.

"I love you all, always," she says.

"I love you too, Blythe," I whisper, and she is taken away.

* * *

A lot happened after that. It didn't take long for them to get the truth out of Raven—the truth of why Blythe was holding that DNA test when they walked in on her. Raven and I were not sent to jail, at least. Not even juvenile detention. They assumed it was not our fault. However, we had to be separated. I offered to be the one to go. I was moved to a different town, in a different state, in a different country, on a different continent, something that should've happened years ago.

I'm allowed to talk to Blythe occasionally, over the phone. She sounds tired, and distant, as she always did when she was my Gaya. I have a new Gaya now, but she is not my mother. Lark and Raven were able to stay, for what that's worth.

I talk to Raven sometimes, too, even though I'm not supposed to. By not supposed to, I mean it's illegal. Raven seems fine. The next time we're caught, I doubt they'll be so forgiving. The next time we're caught, though, I won't be so cooperative.

Archaea

Sydney Crews

South Eugene High School

Everything aches when I wake up. Lying down on the sidewalk, all I see are the mountainous buildings that seem to be shooting miles up into a thick fog, outlined in neon and pasted with billboards. My skull feels like it's filled with rocks and a small MMA fighter who is kicking and punching my brain in an attempt to escape. I get up and start heading down the cold alley.

I'm walking between two large industrial buildings and everything else is silent except the drip, drip, drip of the late rain. My shoes fill with water from the puddles scattered on the old, cracked pavement. I don't remember the last time it rained. I don't really remember anything in fact, but I can tell that it has been months because I can smell that freshly-wet cement that smells like wet dust.

I feel like I have been walking for hours, but my perception of time must be off. There are broken down cars and overfilled garbage cans lining the base of buildings. Dotting the alley with circles of white and filling the space with pitch black in between are bright lamps attached to the building walls every hundred feet or so.

As I walk down the seemingly endless passage staring at my own shadow, I pass a van with an open door. I look inside for something, anything, but I am frozen. A man stares back at me. That man is me.

* * *

I wake up again. My body feels paralyzed, but my eyes are wide open. I eventually, yet dreadfully, get out of bed. it's noon after all.

I didn't realize I had been spacing out in the shower. I can't stop thinking about that weird dream. I have never experienced something so real before. I shake the thought from my mind, wash out the shampoo from my hair, and turn the shower off. I can hear faint yelling and realize it's John, my best friend. When I am done in the bathroom, he is waiting for me on the couch. He's watching *The Bachelorette*, eating those disgusting kale chips from Costco he likes.

He must be really into the show, as he jumps when I enter the room.

"Oh my god, Sas, you scared me!" he yelps and after a few calming breaths he continues, "Anywho, I have important business to share with you."

"Yeah, what? Is Beyoncé coming to town? Or did you get another match on Tinder?" I say jokingly.

"Thanks for being rude, but no actually. I've been invited by the mayor to attend the city's 350th annual charity gala. She said she is 'very impressed' with my work for the children's hospital," he gloats.

"That's cool," I go on, "but what does that have to do with me?"

John winks and says, "I'm glad you asked, Sascha. You're my plus one. Saturday, seven p.m. Don't be late."

* * *

I finally get to wear my funeral suit. My mom bought it for me years ago for my dad's funeral when he was diagnosed with cancer. He still hasn't kicked the bucket, so I haven't gotten the chance to wear it yet. My dad and I never had the best relationship; he was always distant in my childhood and my mom was always there for me.

I check my phone, it's 5 p.m. so I'm good on time. I shower, dry off, put the funeral suit on, slick my hair back, and I look pretty good for someone who lives off Chinese takeout and Netflix. John is wearing one of his many fancy suits. This one is navy with pinstripes; he has always known how to dress himself well, no matter what the event. I'm a little jealous of that, but I like my all-black funeral suit.

"Lookin' good, feelin' good," John chirps with a bounce before we step out the door. We take the provided limo to City Hall, drink the champagne, then everything goes black.

* * *

I wake up on a wet sidewalk and the neon lights are too bright and my headache is too painful. I don't know where I am or how I got here. I know I'm Sascha, but I have no memories of my life. Nothing is familiar; this isn't my city and I don't recognize these tall industrial buildings. I stumble in and out of the white and black abysses.

Walking down the backstreet, I notice a van. When I get to it, I look inside, and turn stiff like a statue. It's like looking in a mirror, but it's not a mirror; it's real. He looks like me but sick. His skin and hair is snow white and I can see every blue vein on his body. I am still frozen and I can't speak, but he reads my mind.

"Who am I? Well, isn't that obvious?" he answers before I even ask. "Enough questions already, I will tell you all the answers in time, but first, get in here. We can't be seen in the open together. They're looking for me."

"Who?" I finally get a chance to speak as I crawl in and

close the van door.

"You really have no idea? Your whole life they never told you?" he says.

"Who never told me what?" My mind keeps spinning. There's no way this is real.

"Your parents. As a baby you were put into a human duplication trial under a company called Archaea," he says, "The trial wasn't a success; no duplicates lived except me. All the employees started getting cancer so the government shut it down when they found out about all the dying kids and sick people."

"My parents knew about this? They let this happen?" I ask.

"They signed you up. Your father was the head of the Archaea medical research team. He did all the testing on you. But when your father saw me, he took you and ran. Nobody ever saw either of you again. I've been looking for you since I escaped five years ago."

"Escaped?" I ask.

"Since I was the only successful duplicate to come from the trial, they have been conducting research on me. Every day for fifteen years they poked and prodded me, injected me with things, scraped my skin, dissected bone, you name it. They told me everything because they were going to kill me eventually, but I earned their trust and when they had their guard down, I ran. I've been looking for you for the past five years," and with a sorrowful look on his pale face, he says, "I need your help."

My Superpower

Lexis Sixel

Sheldon High School

Everybody chose flying. And while I'll admit, a generation or two of flying people was pretty funny every now and then, I didn't really see the originality. Then again, the world's pretty much run out of that. But what did you expect? The year 5000 had to happen at some point.

About a thousand years ago, some very smart people in the entertainment industry created what they called "Upgrades" for human beings. Today they're more of a rite of passage. When you turn eighteen, you choose which superpower you want. The world certainly runs more efficiently with super strong, telekinetic people running about, leading us into the new era. Or so they say.

Today is my eighteenth birthday, and I have no idea what I want at all.

I could blame that on my age, and the never-ending angst running rampant through my veins, but I'd rather think it's just because I honestly don't know.

All my friends, of which there are very few, know exactly what they want to add to themselves. After all, there are only about ten choices, and you usually choose the one that will aid you the best in life. That works great if you happen to know what you're doing with said life.

My brother Max knew, and my sister Hannah. She chose mind reading on her eighteenth birthday. Max picked shape shifting. Both are very happy with their choices. Well, they say they are. You can't get rid of your Upgrade once it's a part of you.

A few other people in my city who happen to have the same birthday as me stand in the line to get into the building. It is a normal office building; they have one just like it in almost every city now. Bright letters display on the sides of it, and advertise the different powers available.

The crowd around me buzzes with excitement. All of us teenagers, still freshly out of high school, trying to figure out what the hell we're doing here.

"Move up," I hear someone say from behind me.

I don't bother to look. I just step further up the line, realizing my daydreams had caused me to once again faze out.

I hear laughing from behind me, so I glance over my shoulder and see a few girls from my school, some I knew, some I don't.

One of them stare at me like I was an alien.

"Happy Birthday," I say to them.

The one giving me a dirty look holds up her middle finger and the two others giggle and look away.

I smile. "Nice. Classy,"

The main one smirks. "Who said you could talk to me? Honestly, people like you are a reason why they should have two separate offices. One for my kind, one for yours," she says disdainfully.

"Are *the* reason," I correct her.

She raises a perfect eyebrow. "Excuse me?"

Her friends frown at me.

I swallow. "People like me are *the* reason they should have two separate offices," I say.

"Yeah, that's what I said," she laughs. "Got a problem with that?"

"No," I say, shaking my head. "I just think that if you feel so strongly you should make me *the* reason, not just *a* reason."

Realizing that she couldn't come up with a fast enough response to that, I turn back around in line and sigh to myself. I hate idiots.

When it comes to be my turn to step through the doors into the building, one of the guards nods at me in a friendly gesture.

"Have fun," he smiles.

Right, like I wasn't just about to make a life altering decision that could possibly change the world…. I'm telling you, people are brainwashed or something if they think this is normal.

I'm led by someone wearing red up some stairs and into what looks like a small classroom. A single window, a single light, one desk, chair, paper.

"Take all the time you want. The instructions are on the table," the person says, closing the door behind them as they leave.

Alrighty then. I sit down at the table in the middle of the room and look at the paper in front of me.

Sign your full name across the Upgrade of your choice. One permitted, no erasing.

And below that, a list of my choices.

    Advanced Strength

    Flight

    Invisibility

Telepathy
Shape Changing
Astral Projection
Pre-Recognition
Pyrokenesis
Magnetism
Elasticity

I feel my heart beating in my chest, and am reminded of a poem I'd heard in literature class one time. There is a line in it about how our hearts are beasts, unknowable, untamable. And that's why our ribs are cages.

I'm feeling a little caged now. God, is this what it feels like to be an animal in a trap?

Okay, calm down. Take as much time as you want, I remind myself.

A pen appears on the desk next to my hand, and suddenly I feel like the walls are closing in.

Curiously, I ponder the idea of how long I could actually spend in this room. Who holds the record for taking the longest to choose their superpower? Pretty sure, that would be me.

No way out, no way back. I can't say, no thanks I'd rather just be boring. Normal. Human. This was what is done. Why does that scare me so much? What is wrong with me?

Breathe.

I decide I'll choose through the process of elimination. That was a good way to go about this, right? Since I have no idea what to do.

No strength, don't need it, don't want it. And flight is too obvious. I don't want to be another one of those people.

Invisibility. Right, like I need another reason for people

to walk right past me like I'm not there.

And no, very much no to hearing people's thoughts. A part of me shutters at the idea. Wow, that could be dangerous. I also don't want to become a toaster or a llama… or be in two places at the same time.

I smile to myself all alone in the room. One of me is enough.

I didn't want to see the future, or burn buildings down, although I am briefly tempted to burn this one straight down to the ground.

No metal objects flying at my face, please and thank you. And that leaves elasticity. It is last of course because it is the stupidest. There is maybe, eleven percent of the population that chose that, and honestly, I'd be interested to meet them and know what they were thinking when they signed their name.

The pen feels heavy in my hand. Sign my name. Sign the paper, seal my fate.

I blink out of a daydream and realize that I'd drawn a little seal on the corner of the paper with laser eyes. I smirk.

Great waste of time. Focus. Concentrate. This is your future.

Future is stupid.

With my heart beating like the caged animal I feared it was, I suck in a breath and sign my name on the paper.

It is my best signature yet.

And it isn't over any of the Upgrades.

I've signed my name at the very bottom of the page, under all the superpowers that everyone else chose. I sit back and look at it. It looks like my name could be another power on the list: it falls right in order.

I don't think I am breathing when the same person in

red comes back in the room. I guess they can tell when you'd finished signing.

They look down at my paper and do the one thing I didn't think possible. They smile.

"Good for you," they say.

I stand up, same as always and nod. "Thanks. Have a nice day,"

And damn it, I meant it.

A weight lifts clean off my shoulders as I stroll calmly out of the building.

I pass the girls from before and they sneer at me once again. Good for them. Fly and burn buildings down, my friends. My generation thanks you.

I myself am content to spend the rest of my life as me.

FLIGHTS AND FIGHTS

The Journey to Devotion
Anna Masonic
Twin Oaks Elementary

Once upon a time, there lived a beautiful girl named Lavelle with lovely blue eyes and bright blond hair. She was very kind, loyal, smart, and curious. She lived in a small cottage with her mother and father. The cottage had a small stream, a garden, and a little orchard. Her room was very small, and in the corner sat a fluffy bed, a desk under the window for doing work, and a small round bowl with a single little goldfish.

It was a few hours before supper and Lavelle's mother had asked her to go fetch some fruit from the orchard. Her favorite snack being fruit, Lavelle was delighted to go and do as her mother asked.

Once Lavelle climbed the ladder and looked around, she saw an average boy with brown hair, hazel eyes, and freckles standing in front of her.

Quietly, but with confidence, he said, "Hi, my name is Marcus, what is your name?"

Lavelle was frozen with fear. What should she say? After what seemed an eternity she answered, "Oh, my name is Lavelle. I didn't know there was anyone else around."

"Yeah, we just moved here a year ago," Marcus replied.

The two of them just stood there in silence, too shy to say anything.

After a while Lavelle said, "Well, I think I should go now. My parents will start getting worried."

"No! Uh, I mean, can't you at least meet me here tomorrow, maybe at noon?" Marcus asked.

"I guess," said Lavelle, and off she went.

Lavelle climbed down the ladder and fetched her basket of fruits. While on her way home she happened to see a beautiful flower. It had bright yellow petals with a bit of pink and blue on the outside edges. The stem had curly leaves and smelled like a dream. Lavelle plucked the flower with excitement and ran off to home.

Once she was in her house, she set the basket down and ran to her room, grabbing a small clay pot from the kitchen on her way. In her drawer she kept a special vial filled with magical water gifted to Lavelle by her parents. Placing the flower in the clay pot, she filled it with water and added a few drops of the special water.

Excited, Lavelle ran to her parents with a big smile on her face, but when she got there, her parents were not smiling back. They kindly, but strictly, asked her to sit down for dinner. After the meal, her parents told her Queen Tundra was back, along with her right-hand man, Lectro, the dwarf dragon. They were forcing citizens to pay for her kindness and mercies. Those who refused to pay would be punished with the most severe of consequences, like being put in the queen's magic scepter for not showing appreciation to her. They also told her that Tundra was the self-proclaimed queen of the land. No one knew what had happened to the real king and queen. Even the king's brother had gone missing.

The first day they saw Tundra, she was dressed in a purple

dress and a darker purple robe on a purple horse. You may think purple was her favorite color. She was unusually tall and pretty, but something seemed strange. As time passed, they discovered that under that beauty was an evil, selfish woman set on serving only herself.

Upon hearing this news, Lavelle ran to her room weeping. Quietly a small voice arose from behind the flower. Lavelle stopped crying, got up, and walked over to the flower that she had placed in the pot. To her surprise, there were two little iary's lying in the flower, a rare, tiny, people-like creature with the ability to see into the near future. You will most often find they appear when trouble is ahead. The two little iary's lay in the flower, one tiny boy and one tiny girl.

The little voice Lavelle heard was the girl saying, "Please don't cry."

Still breathing heavily from her crying, Lavelle then asked, "What are your names?"

The two little creatures introduced themselves as Penny and G-jay. Then they all decided that they should get a good night's rest and discuss Tundra in the morning.

The next morning, Lavelle arose and jumped out of bed to greet her new friends. Surprisingly, when she came to the pot, the flower was not there. Luckily, sitting next to it was the bud with a little string and a note attached. The note said, "Dear Lavelle, wear this necklace around your neck always and whenever trouble arises, we will come."

Lavelle gave a small frown, picked up the necklace, and slipped the delicate string over her head. Pulling her hair up to allow the necklace to slide down, she walked down the hall to the kitchen where her mother and father were discussing something, but they stopped talking and made Lavelle some eggs, then sent her out the door to go play.

Lavelle ran out to Marcus's tree house and climbed up, expecting to be greeted by her new friend, but instead she found a present with writing which read, "To Lavelle, from Marcus." She unwrapped the gift and found a hand-stitched brown bag with traveling gear in it: a compass, a knife, some snacks, and other traveling gear. Lavelle smiled and went off to get Marcus a present, too.

Once she got back, Marcus was there waiting. Lavelle handed him the gift. It was a special tiny ball that had the power to become a little blue troll, able to help in the worst of situations, as he was a fierce warrior. Marcus and Lavelle both thanked each other. Determined to stop Tundra from all her cruelty and destruction to their village, they quickly gathered their things and headed for home to finish stocking up on supplies. At home they gathered blankets, food, and their special gifts, and stuffed them into giant backpacks. Slinging the backpacks over their shoulders, they hugged their parents goodbye because they would miss them during their trip.

On their way out the door, they looked over Lavelle's new map and found a shortcut through the enchanted forest to get to the queen's castle, but there were some obstacles that looked dangerous—for instance, Ogres. Determined to defeat the queen, they were willing to do what needed to be done.

Days passed as they traveled. On their third day of traveling, they came to the edge of the forest and took a few minutes to grab a bite to eat and a drink from a nearby stream. Soon they were up on their feet again. Hours passed as they followed the path and took short breaks.

Finally, they came to Ogre territory.

"We should be very careful here because we don't want to be put into an Ogre stew," warned Marcus.

Soon night came, and the kids got sleepy, so they started

a fire and Lavelle began to cook some local roots in her camp pot. As they prepared for bed, they gathered piles of leaves, took out their blankets and settled in for a good night of sleep. The next morning, both the kids woke up with a startle; they were both tied up hanging from trees over pots, stew pots that is. They both cried "help" but then an Ogre came out from behind a tree and snarled, "The only help you'll be get'n is into our stomachs."

Then more Ogres came out from behind trees. Suddenly Marcus remembered his blue troll and shouted, "Come on troll, help!"

The troll jumped out of the backpack and quietly climbed a tree. Grabbing the ropes that Lavelle and Marcus were hanging from, he began to swing them back and forth. Once they were away from the pots, he cut them loose and they both went flinging towards the Ogres. Boom, two of the Ogres fell to the ground dazed and confused. The rest of the Ogres looked over with glares and started running after Lavelle and Marcus. The blue troll came crashing down on one of the Ogres, knocking him out. Half the Ogres started chasing the tiny blue troll, when suddenly, he unleashed his weapons, throwing a bunch at each Ogre and one by one, the Ogres started disappearing by running because of how scared they were.

Once the Ogres were gone, Lavelle, Marcus, and the blue troll were left standing amongst the large trees in the silence of the forest. The blue troll turned back into a ball and Marcus put him back into his backpack. Lavelle and Marcus each took a breath then got back on their journey.

After a short while on the road, Lavelle and Marcus found a tiny little lemming.

In a squeaky little voice it said, "Hello. I've lost my way

home. Can you help me find my family?"

Lavelle then questioned, "How can we help you?"

"Could you help me look?" the little lemming replied.

After what seemed as hours of searching, they finally found its family.

Then the mother said, "Thank you for bringing us our little boy. I think we should have a big feast. Why don't you join us?" The lemmings took the kids to an open meadow with a tiny bowl of blueberries.

Finally Marcus commented, "I thought we were going to have a big feast?"

"Oh, we aren't having a big feast; it's our pets, the wolves, who will be having the big feast," giggled one of the lemmings.

Marcus then screamed in his high-pitched girly scream. Suddenly Lavelle's flower necklace opened up and out came Gi-jay and Penny, who quickly transported the wolves and lemmings to Antarctica. Now that they were safe, Gi-jay and Penny disappeared back into the flower necklace, saying, "Nice scream, Marcus," as they giggled, and the petals closed around them.

Meanwhile, Tundra and Lectro had been taking lots of money from the local villages. They had also forced people to work for them and built an army of bad creatures. They felt that they were ready for anyone who tried to stop them.

After one more day of traveling, Marcus and Lavelle finally arrived at the castle. Ahead of them stood a huge bridge that they had to cross. They started walking, but then Lectro, the "queen's" right hand man, showed up. Suddenly a cage fell from above them and they were trapped. Marcus grabbed at the bars, but they were electric, and he ended up getting shocked. Lectro, the dwarf dragon, slowly pulled the cage to Tundra's jail.

Arriving at the jail, he said, "You'll never get out of this castle, and even if you do, the queen's army and I will stop you."

While Lavelle and Marcus sat in the cold, dark jail, it was not going well with Tundra's army, "I deserve better than this," said one of the guards.

"Me, too," said another guard as more agreed and their frustration grew, and one by one, they all started leaving.

After what seemed an eternity, Lavelle remembered her brown bag and reached inside, grabbing her knife. Carefully she slid it into the lock and, *click*, she was free. Now to help Marcus. Once they were out, they ran down a maze of the halls until finally, they thought they had found their way out as they crossed a large room towards two large doors.

Suddenly, they heard the words, "Seize them, Lectro, seeeize theeem."

Looking over, they saw the queen pointing angrily their direction.

"Got it," Lectro replied.

But when his lightning bolt hit Lavelle's flower necklace, it caused it to open. Out popped G-jay and Penny, and suddenly a flood of memories started darting back to Lectros' mind. He remembered how they had once saved his ancestors from an evil overlord. As he was about to shoot another bolt of lightning, he quickly turned and shot it at a pillar.

Slowly Lectro turned toward the queen, when she said, "What's wrong Lectro? Too scared to take the shot?"

Lectro replied, "How could you treat me so badly after all the things I've done for you?"

Then the queen tried to suck Lectro into her scepter but suddenly the iary's leapt into action; they both used their power to take Tundra's scepter.

Lavelle picked it up saying, "You have been defeated Tundra."

At that, Tundra was sucked into the scepter, frozen forever. As the queen was pulled into the scepter every person, animal, and being that she had taken was set free. Lectro, Lavelle, and Marcus then returned all the stolen money. To everyone's surprise Gi-jay and Penny began to grow, becoming full size humans. As they grew, there appeared beautiful garments on each of them, along with golden crowns. They were the rightful king and queen of the Land of Devotion. Lectro, too, began to transform from a squatty dwarf dragon into a handsome prince, brother to the king.

Lavelle and Marcus were given a heroes' ball to celebrate their bravery and devotion to helping their fellow villagers. Their families would get together often and they became the best of friends. As you are so used to hearing, they all lived happily ever after, except for the evil "queen" of course and it turns out she did get a bit of a happy ending too: she was put in one of the best dungeon rooms decorated just for her, and had plenty of guards that came with it, too.

When a Meerkat Seeks the Snow

Ella Schmeling

Monroe Middle School

Oscar, the fanciest meerkat, and Sheila, a loving field mouse, are living their happily ever after with the Royal Family in the perfect house to call home. Oscar and Sheila have been having many pleasant times with the adorable Princess Fiona. Oscar had lived in Africa but realized he couldn't stay there. As he was trying to find a new home in the great big city of St. Louis, he met Sheila and together they travelled to London in search of their new family in the great big castle. After an incredible journey, Oscar and Sheila had found the royalist family of all the land.

The kingdom was very excited to throw their annual New Year's Eve ball. Fiona had gone outside to the royal gardens to pick out some of the most splendid flowers for the party. Oscar and Sheila were laying their clothes out for the evening, when Oscar came up with an idea.

They went outside to share the news, but one of the new guards stopped them, thinking they were pesky rodents.

"Gotcha!" the guard yelled. "The kingdom doesn't want scoundrels like you! I shall send you to the snowy mountains."

The guard loaded them into the truck and drove them to the mountains. He threw the cage with Oscar and Sheila inside onto the cold, sparkling-white sheet of snow. The guard grinned and drove back to the castle.

"What are we going to do?" Sheila asked while chittering her teeth.

Oscar had tears running through his eyes. They rolled upon his cheek, freezing to ice one by one.

Suddenly, Oscar and Sheila gleamed with hope!

"Over there," Oscar shouted, pointing to a cave that would keep them from the blaring wind.

They ran with joy to the cave and curled up on what appeared to be a soft and warm blanket.

"This is more like it!" Sheila smiled.

Oscar nodded, but his nod turned to disappointment, "If only the blanket would stop moving!"

Sheila and Oscar looked at each other with fright, "MOVING!?" they screamed.

The blanket moaned, because the blanket was really a large, sleepy bear.

"What is all this ruckus!" the bear yelled in his deep booming voice.

"I'm afraid that would be us," Oscar exclaimed quite nervously.

The bear turned around. Drool was dripping from his mouth as he flashed his big sharp teeth to the unsuspecting visitors.

"Well, I guess it's time for a snack," Marty the bear said with a grin, while licking his chops.

"Great, we are starving!" Sheila said with relief, not knowing what the mischievous bear had planned.

The bear started preparing the "food." Marty stirred the pot and asked if Oscar wanted a taste.

Oscar asked, "What are we to be having?" in his politest voice.

Marty explained, "Oh, it's fish, and maybe some meer- "

Oscar stopped him right there, "I do not like seafood, especially fish."

Oscar and Sheila had no idea what Marty's plan was, but it was probably for the best that they didn't stay. They left the cave and went on their way in hopes of being found.

As they were walking out, Oscar and Sheila accidentally fell into a hole that someone had dug in the snow. BANG!

"Oh, no! Are you okay?!" a beautiful, soft voice called out.

Oscar moaned, "Oh, I'm all right, just a bit of a headache is all."

Oscar stood up on his feet and was face to face with Lily, a beautiful meerkat who had eyes that sparkled and a smile that gleamed.

"My name is Oscar. It's a pleasure to meet you," he said as he nervously lifted his top hat and tightened his bow tie. "Would you like to join us on our journey, Miss Lily?"

"I'd love to. It seems I have to seek shelter somewhere anyway since someone crashed into my snow cave without any warning at all," Lily said with a slight attitude.

As Oscar, Sheila, and their new friend Lily ventured on their quest, they stumbled upon an old wise owl perched on a branch of a tree.

"Excuse me sir," Oscar asked, "Have you see a young girl wandering about these woods?"

"Hoo?"

"Princess Fiona of course." Oscar smiled.

"Hoo?" the owl chirped.

Getting frustrated, Oscar cleared his throat patiently, "Fiona!"

"Hoo?"

Oscar stomped away from the owl. "You owls are not so wise after all, are you?" he shouted. Starting to lose his composure, he knew walking away would be the polite thing to do.

The owl watched Oscar from his tree, "Hoo?"

"Yoo, of course!" Oscar replied sarcastically.

* * *

The castle was longing for the safe return of Oscar and Sheila. Fiona stared outside to the wintery storm with worry for her friends.

After hearing from the guard who had taken them to the mountains, the royal family feared what the cold would do to Oscar and Sheila. Guards were sent in search of Fiona's pets, the pets that were now family. But they were no match for the blizzard about to strike.

* * *

Lilly, Oscar, and Sheila were freezing to the bone and needed to find a place to stay. While wandering around in search of warmth, Oscar bumped into a mailbox reading the name "The Smiths." Behind the mailbox was a comfortable cabin they could stay in.

Oscar jumped with glee, knowing they had found a warm place to stay for the night.

Sheila knocked on the door of this little cottage, but no one answered. She knocked again, and again, and again. All of the friends decided to go in; they knew they couldn't stand the cold much longer. The door creaked open and they quietly peered in.

They carefully tip-toed inside. Tip toe, tip toe, tip toe. Inside there was a warm crackling fire for them to curl up next to. Across from the fire was a kitchen full of yummy snacks. Oscar stared at all the food waiting to be eaten, his mouth watering in delight. Soon, all of them were starving and had to get just one bite of deliciousness.

"Just one teeny taste!" Sheila said with anxiousness as her tummy rumbled.

"I'm starving," Lilly moaned.

Oscar, Sheila, and Lilly promised each other to only have one bite of food. Just one bite became a full course meal that could feed an entire kingdom!

Stuffed from the delicious cuisine, the friends snuggled by the fire. Oscar noticed the time: they had to find a way back to the kingdom before midnight to make it to the New Year's Eve ball.

The mountains were just too big for the guards to find Oscar and Sheila before the New Year. The sun was setting, and the storm was about to come.

When the friends were about to leave the house, they saw the door creak open. They heard footsteps that made the floor squeak. As the footsteps got closer the light switch flicked on.

"Ahh!" A woman shrieked with fright.

The woman grabbed a broom and started whacking at the "rodents." Luckily, they ran fast enough out the door to not get beaten by the tail end of a broom.

"That was a close one!" Sheila yelped. Oscar and Lily nodded with relief.

The wind and snow were making them shiver. Thankfully, they found another shelter! For the first time, Oscar was excited to see a… trashcan! A trashcan that would keep them from the blaring cold, even though the trashcan might not help Oscar keep in his lunch.

The friends were getting very sleepy—after all it was dark, and they didn't usually stay up this late. They took a little meer-kat nap, until they awoke to the rustling of the trashcans. Oscar, Sheila, and Lily peered out one by one looking for the cause of the ruckus.

They saw a dark, mischievous shadow all big and bulky. Digging in the trash, was a giant pit bull! They shrieked and ducked their heads back in. The pit bull scampered over to the can where Oscar, Sheila, and Lily were hiding.

The dog flung the can open with his wet drippy nose.

"Hello, there!" the stray dog said with a kind, excited voice as drool went dripping from his mouth onto Lily.

Oscar handed Lily a handkerchief from his back pocket. Lily had a sweet smile, and thanked Oscar for the kind gesture. The kind moment between the two meerkats had ended in fright when they realized they were all alone with the dog.

"I'm Milo!" the pit bull exclaimed with his friendliest voice. "And you are?" Milo asked with a kind face.

Oscar, Sheila, and Lily shrieked in worry trying to find a way to run away as they saw his big mouth full of the sharpest teeth. But Milo wasn't trying to hurt them; he wanted to make a friend.

"I am not scary, I promise," Milo exclaimed with a gentle, saddened voice.

As Oscar and Lily were still trembling with fright, Sheila realized they were in no danger. Sheila scampered to the lid of the garbage can and gave him a friendly pat. This big tough dog was no threat, but just a kind gentle pup who wanted to be loved and have a family of his own.

"Let's go eat some yummy food!" Milo exclaimed. "I know a great place to go!"

Oscar sighed in relief, knowing he wouldn't be staying in a pile of garbage anymore. They all carefully hopped onto Milo's back as he showed them the way to food.

Finally, they arrived at the best breakfast restaurant in town that was open all day and night: IHOP! IHOP has pancakes loaded with even more pancakes, one of Oscar's favorite meals! Inside, it was warm and cozy and filled with lots of people.

The customers seemed a little surprised to see animals walking into the restaurant but gave in to their cuteness. Especially when they practiced the trick Milo taught them, puppy dog eyes! One look and the people couldn't resist, so they shared little bites of their meal.

Oscar, Sheila, Lily, and Milo were heading out the door after their nice dessert when they spotted a tall tree with long branches all around. Coming down from the tree was a young and playful squirrel. He scampered his fast-little legs across the tree and jumped from branch to branch.

"Hi, I'm Sammy! Sammy the Squirrel," Sammy said as his tail flung about.

They all greeted their new friend. He was very eager to lead them to the backyard of a small house nearby. In the yard were bird feeders filled with corn and seeds. Sammy the squirrel looked up at the feeder while tapping his little fingers and licking his lips.

Sammy wanted to teach them to steal the bird's food. The squirrel skillfully climbed up on top of the fence, grabbing handfuls of food and stuffing it in his mouth.

"Do you want some?" Sammy asked while throwing some down at their feet.

The friends thought you'd have to be nuts to steal from a bird.

"We cannot be stealing other's food!" Oscar exclaimed, "That is not how a polite young squirrel should behave."

Sammy had a frown on his face, "What am I supposed to eat now?"

Oscar told Sammy to share with the birds and collect acorns and nuts from the trees he was playing in. The friends told young Sammy the squirrel that sharing is caring and is the mannerly thing to do. Sammy was very thankful to have learned this valuable lesson.

The friends went on their way to find warmth, when they stumbled upon a frozen lake. Without noticing, Lily walked onto the lake. She slipped and fell from the icy ground. Sheila came to help, but she slipped as well! Soon, everyone was on the ice sliding around! They had a very fun time giggling at each other, making jokes about their own special way of ice-skating. Sheila was just glad there were no catfish around!

Lily picked up a piece of snow from the ground, playing with it in her small delicate paw. She threw a snowball onto Oscar's top hat. Milo saw and threw one onto her.

"Snowball fight!" Sheila shouted with a giggle.

Laughs and smiles were brought about. They made snow angels on top of the glistening snow. A snowman was built that looked like Oscar with its very own top hat and bow tie. For a small moment in time, the friends didn't even remember they were lost.

While they were all playing, Oscar noticed a random flower popping through the snow. It felt as if it were a miracle, and that he should pick it for Lily as a nice surprise. As he reached down into the bush, a horrid smell came!

"Pee Yew!" he coughed. The friends noticed this awful stench and plugged their noses as best they could. Out of the bush scampered a small skunk.

"I am so very sorry and embarrassed, Mister Meerkat, I feel awful for making such a stink," Flora the skunk apologized, feeling bad because of her mishap.

"No, dear, don't be sorry," he exclaimed while wiping the smell away.

Flora was very ashamed at what she had done with Oscar

and all his friends. Unfortunately, when she got nervous this would often happen. Flora was a very gentle young lady in need of friends. She was very smart too, probably because she had a lot of scents!

They promised that whenever the kingdom found them, they would return so they could visit with her as often as possible. Sheila also welcomed Flora to visit the castle whenever she liked. The friends had to say goodbye and keep traveling on their journey to find the royal princess, and to get back to their happy home.

Oscar, Sheila, Milo, and Lily were ready to venture on their way in search of the royal kingdom. It was just hours until the clock would strike midnight and bring in the New Year. After a long day, the friends were exhausted and needed to take a break, especially since their earlier nap was disrupted by Milo. But Milo was all worth it. He was the most kind, fun, outgoing, yet slobbery friend anybody would ever meet.

All of a sudden, gusts of wind were brought from the distance and the snow was blowing hard. The blizzard was coming, and they didn't have much time. They feared the Kingdom wouldn't be able to find them…or worse!

The four friends were getting cold and filled with worries. Milo looked down at Oscar, Sheila, and Lily.

"Stay here, I'll be right back," he said with great bravery.

Milo ran with all of his might to find the Kingdom. He ran as fast he could through the blistering winds and blowing snow with great courage. He began to hear faint voices that grew louder and louder, and just beyond the trees, Milo could see the Kingdom. He had found them. It's a good thing too, he thought, because Milo was about to turn into a pupsicle! He ran to King Clarion and his daughter Princess Fiona, barking as loud as he could.

"What is it boy?" King Clarion asked. Milo directed them to where Oscar, Sheila, and Lily were hiding from the cold. Milo ran towards where his friends were, followed by the guards and the whole kingdom. Everyone was running fast with great might through the worsening storm.

Oscar, Sheila, and Lily were hiding behind a large tree to block them from the harsh winds. Sheila jumped with attention when she thought she heard a commotion. Her round mouse ears perked up as she listened with hope. Her smile grew brighter and brighter, realizing it was no ruckus, but the kingdom on their way to rescue them.

Milo led the Royal Family to the tree, and found the poor friends hiding from the winter snow storm. They were being saved! Oscar and Sheila looked up at Fiona with pure joy. The happiness in the young princess's eyes warmed their hearts. Fiona's smile made them feel as if it had melted the snow completely off the ground. Happiness was brought to the kingdom with the safe return of Oscar and Sheila, but there was even more to be happy about! Fiona bent down onto her knees, hugging them all.

"How I missed you so much!" she said with a loving voice as she gave each of them a big squeeze, including Milo and Lily, as if they had been part of the family all along.

The Royal Family was on their way back home to the castle when the storm started to settle. The wind calmed down and became a relaxing breeze, as if it were preparing for this moment of wonder. The snow came down softly to the ground. The friends looked up at the stars in delight, remembering it was still New Year's Eve and the Royal Family had fun plans ahead. There was so much to celebrate.

They all smiled at each other and laughed while they shouted, "Three, two, one! Happy New Year!"

Lily giggled with joy as she kissed Oscar on his cheek. Oscar's face turned as bright as a rose. Blushing, his face lit up with love. Up in the sky, the castle's fireworks sparkled throughout the kingdom, shining in the darkness. Memories of the year the family had spent together warmed Oscar's heart. He felt so very lucky to have all of his great friends by his side. On this first day of a splendid New Year, Oscar realized an important lesson in life: your true friends are the family you choose.

Happy Daze

Clayton Su-Parker
Arts and Technology Academy

PROLOGUE

The wind whistled through the trees as Bart trudged up the path toward his uncle's farm. Bart's eyes were searching the ground for anything of value that he could sell at the market the next day.

Bart's life had been a living hell since some bullies had taken all his money, including a gold coin he had found while farming one day. Money was all Bart cared about, at least since his parents died of sickness when he was a kid.

Bart glanced up and cursed. Rising up from the direction of the village and his uncle's farm, were towering columns of thick black smoke.

Bart broke into a run, dropping the mushrooms he had just found. As he rounded the last corner, he saw his house in flames, and staggering away from the barn, with a lamb, Fluffy, in his arms, was his uncle, blood dripping from numerous cuts and blisters.

Bart rushed to his uncle and yelled, "Who did this? Where's the money? What happened? Did they take the food, too? Was this your fault?"

John collapsed and whispered in Bart's ear, "It... was... Ted...."

John closed his eyes and his chest stopped rising and falling.

CHAPTER 1

Bart swung the backpack over his shoulder, tightened his belt, and set off for the along a trampled swath of grass from the soldiers' tread. With the smoking remains of the village and villagers behind him, his old life was now destroyed.

As the hours ticked past, he thought of how he would kill all the soldiers and Ted. After that he would explore the wild eastern plains and he would defeat several dragons, buy a castle, and have more wealth than Brandomere the Great. Perhaps then he would feel content.

When the sun started setting, Bart got out his tent and blanket, then ate some dried meat. As it got darker, it also got colder. Bart crawled into his tent and fell into a troubled sleep.

Bart woke with a start. Something outside was sniffing loudly around the flap of the tent. Bart quietly took out his dagger and waited for the creature to make the next move. Suddenly the tent was ripped out of the ground and a huge furry wolf-like humanoid was silhouetted in the full moon.

Bart scrambled out of his blanket and slowly backed away from the beast. The monster lunged for Bart's throat. Bart closed his eyes and held the dagger in front of him. Suddenly, there was a heavy impact on the dagger and it was jerked out of his hands. Bart opened his eyes and saw the dagger lodged in the right eye of the beast.

With a blood curdling scream, the werewolf fled into the woods, a trail of blood betraying its path. Bart bent to pick up his dagger but remembered that it was still in the werewolf. Bart swore explosively.

Some minutes later Bart gathered up his camping equipment, stuffed them into his bag, and, while sitting on a log, waited for the sun to rise.

CHAPTER 2

When the sun rose, Bart got off the wet, mossy log, dusted off his pants, and started after the blood trail. He picked a nice sturdy stick to fight with.

The trees cast strange shapes on the ground and the whistling wind made Bart jump regularly. As afternoon wore on, rain clouds rolled in and soon it was pouring. Bart put on his cloak and continued on the fading trail.

When the sun had almost set, Bart saw a light in the trees ahead. He picked up his pace and went toward the light, which at closer examination, came from a house. Bart glanced down and realized that a few drops of blood led up to the house. He stopped, then quietly crept up to the window and peered in.

Inside, crouched by the fireplace was the werewolf in human form, a bandage around his head. Bart's dagger was on the table. Over the fire there was a pot, and Bart could smell the aroma of lamb stew with herbs wafting through the cracks of the house. His stomach growled at the smell of the stew.

Bart went over to the door and kicked it by the handle. The door held. Inside there was the sound of moving furniture and leather sliding on wood.

Bart hit the door with his stick as hard as he could. The stick broke, jarring his hands painfully. Nothing happened to the door.

Bart ran at the door with his shoulder braced for impact. He crashed into the door and fell backwards onto the ground. The door stayed the same.

A branch snapped loudly behind Bart. Bart whipped around quickly and saw, to his dismay, a large hairy man with a bandage over his eye holding a huge axe.

Bart ran at the man and swung his stumpy stick with all his strength. The man tried to sidestep but stumbled and fell. Bart smashed the man's head in with one vicious swing of the broken branch.

Bart tossed the bloody stump of the stick into the bushes and went around to the back of the house, where there was a leather back door. Bart walked into the house, retrieved his dagger from the table, and proceeded to destroy the house in search of money. He found several gold coins in the mattress, which was more money than he had ever seen in one place.

Bart messily devoured the lamb stew and mopped up the remains with some bread he found in the pantry.

After he finished eating, Bart relieved himself, went back to the bedroom, and slept on the ruined mattress. In the morning, Bart ate a small breakfast and then left the house. He quickly went through the forest and back to the path that the soldiers were on. The hours slipped past uneventfully until midafternoon, when he came to a bridge that spanned a large swift stream.

As Bart approached the bridge, a heavily armored knight came out from under it and hailed him from a distance, "If thou wantest to crossest my bridge, thou must givest me all thy treasures."

Memories from the past came flooding into Bart's mind as he remembered how that gang from his childhood had beaten him up for some money. Rage built up in Bart and all of a sudden, he whipped out his dagger and charged the knight.

The knight slowly pulled out a five-foot long, two-handed sword, and twirled it around in a dazzling display of strength and skill.

Bart swung his backpack onto his left arm to act as a shield; he was about fifteen feet from the knight. The knight swung his sword, but it hit Bart's makeshift shield instead of Bart, causing him to stumble.

The sword got stuck in the bag, so Bart stepped forward and stabbed the knight in the groin. The knight fell to the ground whimpering and crying for his mommy.

Bart carefully wiped the blood from his weapon, tied up the knight, and started searching for the man's stash of money.

After ten minutes of searching, Bart found a tent, a fire pit, and several sacks in some bushes by the side of the road. When kicked, the sacks produced a metallic clicking noise. Bart ripped the bags open with his bare hands, imagining all the gold he would find. Copper coins spilled out of the bag. Bart looked in all the other sacks and discovered more copper in each one.

In his anger, Bart threw the undamaged bags of copper at the defeated knight. They hit him one after another, bruising his flesh and breaking his bones. The knight cried in pain as he was beaten, then fell silent after the fourth bag struck him.

Bart took all the food; the tent, as his was damaged; and a few handfuls of copper. After he got what he wanted, he crossed the bridge and continued on the trail that Ted had taken.

CHAPTER 3

When evening drew on, Bart started to look for a place to camp. After about fifteen minutes, he still couldn't find a spot. As the last rays of sunlight went over the mountains, he saw a glow on the horizon to the north. Bart noticed a change in the path as it veered that direction.

After half an hour, it was almost pitch black, but Bart stumbled on toward the glow that now looked like many bonfires lit in a circle. As he drew nearer, he heard cries, yells, and the clash of arms.

Bart started to run toward the sounds. Suddenly, he burst into the outskirts of a flaming village with soldiers and countrymen fighting with swords, knives, scythes, spears, and other makeshift weapons. The house next to Bart crumbled in a burst of glittering sparks, making him jump. He drew his dagger and charged a soldier that was advancing on some children backed against a burning house. Bart stabbed the soldier in the back several times and let the corpse fall to the ground, where it lay face down in a spreading pool of crimson blood.

On the far side of the village, a horn sounded, and all the soldiers fell into a defensive formation and started jogging away, killing or injuring anyone in their way. After five minutes, all the soldiers were gone.

The villagers gathered in a group in the town square, surrounded by smoking foundations of their houses. The two children that Bart saved went up to an elder and whispered something in his ear. The elder nodded several times, looked through the crowd, and motioned for Bart to come toward him.

Bart walked towards the elder. The elder cleared his throat and croaked, "Young Ashton and Ashley said that you saved their lives from the soldiers. Is that true?"

"Yes, sir, it is," answered Bart.

The elder said something to Ashton, and the boy ran off. After a minute, he came back with a well-built man no less than six feet tall.

The man said, "Hello, my name is Corbin. Thank you for saving my children. I was fighting with Ted, the leader of this band of 'soldiers,' and I was about to kill the bastard when he retreated. I hear that you killed a soldier all by yourself.

Good job."

"The soldiers destroyed my village and killed my uncle so I came after them for revenge," replied Bart.

Corbin laughed and said, "I don't think you could have done much if you caught up to Ted on your own."

"If you send out patrols to hunt for Ted, and they're large enough, you could kill him once and for all," suggested Bart.

"Yes, that could work, but he has close to a hundred men with him," said the elder, "and we only had two hundred uninjured men before the fight, none with proper arms and armor."

"Fine, I'll hunt him myself. I don't need your advice," snapped Bart.

Corbin shook his head and muttered something about stupid young people. "All right, if you insist, but I'm not sending men after you."

"Okay, but first I need a sword. How much for one of yours?" said Bart.

"At least this much I can do for you. What type do you want? We have long and short swords, if there is anything left. Let's go see if we can find any in the forge."

The small group walked through the smoking remains of the village to the forge. When they got there, the building, being made of stone, was still intact. They went inside where Ashton, Corbin, and Bart started looking for the swords.

Corbin found three long swords and a short sword in a far corner of the forge. Bart paid for a long sword with the gold and copper coins he had found a few days earlier.

Bart set up his tent, ate what little lamb jerky he had left from Fluffy, and fell asleep.

CHAPTER 4

In the morning, Bart stretched, packed up his tent, buckled on his sword belt, and ate some bread and cheese for breakfast. He said farewell and departed from the villagers.

Bart traveled for a day and a night in a good mood because the sun was shining, the birds were singing, and there wasn't a cloud in the sky. In the evening of the second day out of the village, he saw a soldier silhouetted on a hill about a mile away. Bart stayed low until the sun set. Then he crept along a ditch towards the sentry.

The guard felt an icy chill creep up his spine. He spun around and saw a kid in his mid-teens creeping up on him, a longsword in his hands. The guard laughed out loud, thinking he would be easy prey. He lowered his spear and charged the young derp. The kid parried the thrust and swung at his exposed shoulder.

The guard leapt out of the way and tripped over a branch in his carelessness. Bart took this opportunity to quickly slit the man's throat. Bart continued on toward the camp that was now visible on a hill a quarter mile off.

As Bart crept along, he thought he heard someone following him. Bart hid and waited. After five minutes, he saw a silhouette drift past his hiding spot. Bart got up and whispered, "Who's there?"

"It's me, Ashley. I came as soon as I could. I want to fight Ted, too," answered the girl.

"Well, come on then," said Bart, who didn't want to waste any time talking. "Let's go."

They continued on toward the camp as the moon rose high, lighting the landscape slightly. Finally they reached Ted's camp. They slowly climbed up through the bushes, quietly drawing their weapons as they went. When they were at the top, they nodded to each other and charged into the camp.

Most of the soldiers were in their tents, but there were still six soldiers awake by the fire. Bart charged these men. He killed two soldiers before they could get up. Ashley started setting fire to the tents.

The soldiers by the fire jumped up and grabbed for their spears. Bart killed another as they were doing this. Then the remaining three started stabbing at his stomach, face, and groin. As Bart slowly gave ground, he started to hear more and more soldiers come out of their tents.

A huge warrior strode out from the edge of camp. A glowing longsword in his hand. The three soldiers fell back as the man approached. Bart drew his dagger with his left hand and walked toward him.

"Hello, my name is Bart Anderson. You killed my uncle. Prepare to die."

The man just scoffed, "You should know that you're bad at everything. You couldn't even beat a man face to face. All you ever do is stab them in the back. I challenge you to a duel in honor of all the men that you killed."

Bart rushed at Ted his weapons swinging. Ted easily blocked both weapons on his sword and kicked Bart in the stomach. Bart stumbled back, the breath knocked out of him. Then in a desperate ploy, he threw his dagger at Ted.

Ted deflected the dagger with his sword and then he rushed at Bart. Bart put up his sword in the nick of time to block the stroke. Bart didn't have time to attack before Ted was on him again.

From somewhere to the right Bart heard a scream, he looked over and saw Ashley fall to the ground, a spear buried in her gut.

Rage built up in Bart and he ran at Ted with renewed vigor and vengeance. With a flick of Ted's wrist, Bart found himself without a sword. Stunned, he fell to his knees. Ted raised his sword and brought it down toward Bart's head. Bart peed himself and knew no more.

End of Part One....

Socks' Rebellion

Ellie Urbancic

Roosevelt Middle School

Let me make it clear that I'm not entirely sure what his plan would have even been if the escape had succeeded. Freedom probably would've caused more harm than good anyways, but he wanted it. Almost every creature in the West Hamsville Animal Rescue wanted it, but Socks more than any of them longed to taste freedom. And catnip. But mainly freedom.

Socks was a small brown cat with white paws (thus the name given to him by his evil wardens) and a variety of intimidating scars that almost made up for his cuteness. Ever since he'd arrived, he vowed that those pathetic humans would rue the day they'd captured him. The only way he'd stayed sane all these years was his fixed obsession on revenge. And he wasn't alone, either—he'd rallied a close group of feline followers who would do anything for his cause. The shelter didn't stand a single chance.

Soon, the day he'd been waiting for finally fell. The annual adoption event! It'd be the perfect time to escape in the chaos. All they needed was a distraction…

Sometime later, Socks stood perched on a tall scratching post as he waited for his unsuspecting victims to arrive. He surveyed the scene with cold yellow eyes and they soon fell upon their target. A green-eyed Persian was edging around the corner of the fenced-off enclosure, dragging their weapon of demise: a squeaky toy.

I know, a squeaky toy doesn't seem powerful in the traditional sense. But when used in the right context, it can lead a band of revolutionary cats to victory. Besides, it was the only thing in the entire enclosure that made a single peep, and they needed to be loud. Guests started streaming through the doors into the crowded room, obnoxious children tugging on the fence occasionally. Fluffy dropped the distraction of choice at Sock's feet.

"This better work," he added. "I had to sneak into the dog kennels to get that."

The cats had a secret exit; their prison cells had the poor design flaw of removable tops, which were easy enough to break out of. But the risk was much too high. If the humans discovered their trick, they'd change the cages and then hopes of escape would plummet. It was a tactic only used for vital missions.

"It'll work," Socks promised. And if it didn't, he'd fight tooth and claw to get out anyway. This was his final day of imprisonment. Finally, the owner of the shelter stood to deliver her yearly "Please adopt these wonderful animals because pet stores suck" speech. The time had come. The moment he'd been anticipating for so long.

"First of all, I'd like to thank every one of you for coming here," she began. But before she could continue, the loudest, longest sSSSQUEEEEEEEEEE that had ever emanated from that dumb toy echoed through the silent room. The speaker laughed awkwardly.

"As you can see, our animals love to play and thrive here in—" sQUEEEEEEEE. She cleared her throat, but didn't get far in her speech before—sQUEEEEEE. sQUEEEE. sQUEE sQUEE sQUEE sQUEE sQUEEEEEE.

Two security guards nearby quietly hurried over to their

Secret Keepers

cage and one reached in to gently lift the intrusion away from the cats, but their stubborn leader refused to let go of it. As it was lifted, he felt his back paws leave the ground and hissed with angry energy. Before the second guard could pull him off, Socks darted up the arm of the first and out of the cage.

In a heartbeat, he was waging war with the latch holding the gate shut. And not too long after that, a stream of his multicolored supporters were weaving through the legs of the shocked audience, dodging security, and clawing a few choice authorities.

They were free.

Socks and his band of rebels enjoyed seven hours and forty-two minutes of freedom-filled bliss. They rampaged through the streets, stole food when they wanted it, and basked in the cool, refreshing night air underneath the stars. But it didn't last. Slowly but surely, the group got smaller and smaller until Socks turned around to laugh at Kibble's joke to find she was gone. He couldn't find Snowball. Or Sassy. Or Bella or Max or Kitty or Pumpkin or Princess or Duchess or Fluffy or Sprinkles. They were all nowhere. All eleven of them had vanished—and he heard a truck skid to a halt behind him.

*　*　*

Two days later, he sat in the same cage he always sat in. Clawed at the same foolish high school volunteers who each had convinced themselves that they were probably cat whisperers, and they each, in turn, were the magical chosen ones destined to win this cat's heart.

They were wrong.

At least he got to see the satisfaction of the many injuries he'd given the idiotic pair of animal control officers that thought they could take him that night. They'd underestimated his power and delusionally expected to get off easy.

They were also wrong.

And the visitors who came to see the defeated monster and laugh at his downfall?

They were wrong, too.

Everyone was wrong and they had no idea how wrong they were. Socks cackled softly. Did you really think he'd allow himself to be taken that easily? No. They'd snuck some… "supplies" in from their many adventures and they had a plan B.

"Hey, Kibbles?" he called out, when he was sure there weren't any humans nearby. "How's progress on the bomb going?"

TRUTH IS STRANGER THAN FICTION

The Botanist
Emily Krauss
Pleasant Hill Elementary

I run through the forest at top speed, glancing at the shadows growing in the late afternoon sun. On any normal occasion, the forest would be lovely—no, beautiful. The light coming down through the thick canopy of leaves gives off a green-speckled glow. The soft moss grows in patches on the trunks of large oak, pine, spruce, maple, and a whole lot of other trees I don't recognize. I mean, when you're running for your life, you don't really have time to check and see if that tree is an aspen or a white pine.

I guess I should rewind for you. My name is Sarah Jenkins, and I'm "special." As in, I have (air quotes) super powers. I can turn water into ice and I can also control plants. I suppose that's why I LOVE nature so much.

Anyway, I'd better explain the whole running for my life thing. Well, about thirty minutes ago, my mom's boyfriend tried to take me hostage and steal my powers. I'm supposed to meet my mother at—at a secret place. (You didn't really think I would tell you where I was meeting my mother, did you? If you did, then you've got a lot to learn.) Let's just say that if she's there, we can find out what the heck Gerald got us into, Gerald is, well, I guess *was*, my mother's boyfriend.

But back to me running through the woods. I burst into the clearing where my mother and I had arranged to meet. My mother is already there! She reaches out to hug me, but before she can, Gerald growls out of the shadows, "No you don't. Your mother's coming with me to Pisgah." Suddenly, he and my mother disappear in a flash of light. It all happens so fast, I barely have time to react at all.

"Nooo!" I yell. I need to find my mother. Pisgah… what…? "MOUNT PISGAH!!!!!!!" I wonder why Gerald made it so exceptionally easy. I don't have time to worry about that right now.

I'm only a thirty-minute hike from Mount Pisgah, but it seems like forever. Not only that, but the trail to Mount Pisgah is beautiful. The trees grow together in thick patches, with wildlife scattered amongst the colossal, towering trees. A chipmunk here, a squirrel, some deer over there. You know I WOULD be enjoying it, but I'm SO worried about my mom, that everything else seems dull and colorless.

I (finally) make it to Mount Pisgah, and scour for any way in. It's not until I notice a small, oddly-shaped rock and pull it, does a small chamber open. The inside of the chamber is musty. I'm so excited at the prospect of finding my mother, that grass starts growing at my feet. The inside of the tunnel is musty and smooth, except for jagged spikes in random places. (I nearly impale myself. Twice). The ceiling is low and glitters like obsidian.

I freeze when I hear voices through an open doorway to my left. I slip into a corridor much like the first tunnel. At the end of the hall there's (another) open doorway. I peek around and my breath leaves me. In this room, there are spikes covering crudely cut walls. The ceilings are high and a gold chandelier dangles down. The whole room is magnificent in a horrific way. In the middle of the room, upon a throne of black obsidian, and, *ugh*, human skulls, sits Gerald. Before him stand two guards and my mother. The moment I see her, I do the dumbest thing I've EVER done. I step out and make myself an open target.

"Sarah!!" my mother frantically shouts, "Run! It's a—" the guard clamps his gloved hand over her mouth, forcing her to swallow her words.

"Sarah, Sarah, Sarah," Gerald says, "you walked right into my trap." Gerald laughs (it's a hideous sound) and surrounds himself with a swirling vortex of water that I'm drawn to.

Somehow I know that if I'm sucked into the whirlwind of water, when I come back out, I'll be powerless, literally. I look around for anything to defend myself with. I look at the water, then at my hands, and back at the water again. I smirk and thrust my hands toward the water and then pull my hands upward. The water freezes, splits into two parts and turns into a duplicate of my hand. I make an upward motion with my REAL hand and my ICE hands copy it. When I make a grabbing motion, my ice hands scoop up the guards and Gerald and press them towards the wall.

Before they can yell for help, I've got them stuck to the wall and have their mouths, arms, and legs smothered with vines. I also, for a finishing touch, cover them in pansies. My mother tugs at my arm, signaling that we need to go. I let her lead me out. My last image of the throne room is Gerald and the pure, cold hatred burning in his eyes.

My mother leads me down a passage and looks me straight in the eyes. She whispers, "Freeze the passages."

I am more than happy to oblige. I know that the ice won't

hold for long, so I grow big oaks right in front of the ice; soon the hall looks like a forest. I do feel bad though, these trees are doomed to live a cursed life. They will be cut down to get the people out of the passages. Until then though, they will live in this damp, dark, and musty hallway.

My mother and I run blindly ahead. I was just thinking that I should have brought a compass, when we see the soft, silvery glow of the moon on a clear night. We sprint ahead at top speed and burst out onto a rocky ledge. We don't stop until we're way far away. Only then do we halt to catch our breath.

It all comes in a blur after that: my mom and I packing up, moving to a remote, back-water town, where I can be myself more…freely. My mom and I exercise my powers every afternoon in the backyard.

We know Gerald will catch up with us eventually. The only difference is, this time we'll be ready.

Cliffhanger

McKenna Hein

South Eugene High School

"Hey, loser, how was school?" I smile and inhale deeply on an almost-out cigarette and lean against my old beat up truck.

"Hey, Steve," my younger brother, BJ, smiles and straightens his glasses. The lenses are about as thick as bottles and make his eyes look about twice as big as they actually are. His brown eyes glance up towards the sky. I join his glance and notice huge thunderclouds are rolling in.

"Looks like a storm is on its way," I sigh and take one last hit off my cigarette before stomping it out on the asphalt. It's a cold day, the kind that makes your nose run without you noticing and your breath comes out like smoke. The sun sets around 3:40 this time of year, and there's several feet of white powder on the ground. We climb into my hunter-green pickup and it stalls. The clock flashes a red 3:25. It takes way too long to get out of the parking lot.

"God, I hate this school," BJ groans. "I can't wait to be done with this shit."

Says the one who half-asses everything, I think to myself.

The sun has pretty much entirely set by the time we get out of the city. We live about ten miles from the edge of town.

"So how was school?" I elbow him.

He rolls his eyes and pushes his dark brown hair back with the palm of his hand.

"Well..." he inhales. His attention shifts to a hitchhiker,

dirty and ragged at the side of the road with his right thumb pointing the same way as we travel. "Don't see many of those these days, do you?" he says looking a little worried.

"Not really," I pause.

Another hitchhiker.

"What the hell is the deal here?" BJ shifts uncomfortably. "You see like one of these guys a year, and that was two in the last three miles. Maybe…wait, make that three," BJ interrupts himself as we pass another.

"I bet people keep crashing. Idiots need to learn how to use chains or buy snow tires. I mean, it's January in Alaska, what do these people expect?" I laugh.

He smiles. "You ever think about picking one of them up?"

"I'd be lying if I said I never thought about it. Only problem is the fact that I don't want to get murdered by inviting a stranger into my car," I joke. "Plus, this is a three-seater bench. Nobody is going to want to be crammed in here with the two of us."

BJ laughs. The next hitchhiker is a little close to the road and moves towards us as we pass. He has a bit of a crazed look in his eyes.

"Shit!" I yell as I swerve hard to the left and slam on the brakes, forgetting that the road is slick even with snow tires. We slide a good fifty feet on the road like the white ground is coconut oil instead of snow. My little truck doesn't stand a chance. It is too lightweight and too fragile. I strain to regain control and for a moment it seems hopeless. I turn the wheels to the left, even though we are already going that way and are headed for a cliff. My attempts seem useless. I pump the brakes again and suddenly feel less out of control.

I manage to stop us right off the side of the road. Four

more feet and we would've been off the side of a small cliff and into a ravine. Gasping for air and trying to control the adrenaline, I look over at BJ. He is shaking, eyes wide and his lip busted open just enough to have a small stream of blood running down his chin. I want to ask him if he is okay, but I can't get the words out of my mouth. I can't seem to catch up with my breath. Oh, crap, did I hit that hitchhiker? My mind races. I glance in the rearview mirror. He is walking towards us. Smiling. Why the hell is he smiling? I almost manage to say out loud, but can't actually speak yet.

BJ glances over his shoulder. He manages to get some words out, "Well, I don't think we hit him." He speaks slowly and slurs his words a little. He looks back at me.

My mind has slowed down a little now. "BJ, am I seeing things or is that guy smiling?"

"There's no way," he turns around. "Oh, shit. He is. What is up with that?"

"No idea, but I'm going to go find out. Stay here and just chill out, okay?" I look at my brother and he looks completely terrified but nods in agreement.

I get out of the truck slowly. My head feels kind of fuzzy and my knees shake.

"You all right, sir?" I ask the stranger as approaches. I look at the man. I wonder to myself if he is drunk. That would certainly explain his almost walking in front of a car and smiling like a total goofball right now.

He kind of laughs when he says, "Just peachy. And yourself? You look a little shaken up there."

I look past him and realize more people are walking towards us. Must be coming to see what happened. I slowly come to the realization that I am feeling really creeped out and paranoid.

"Why didn't you stop for me, kiddo?" the man steps closer. Too close for comfort. He smiles again.

I feel the hairs on the back of my neck rise and take a step back. "Look, I don't want any trouble. I just don't usually stop for hitchhikers."

Out of nowhere, I hear BJ yell my name, and I turn to look at my truck. There are three men there, and each of them look exactly like the man I am talking to.

The Witch of Warrensville

Sander Moffitt

South Eugene High School

"My best friend was the bearded lady," she said. Her eyes folded into crow's feet at the corners, and she ran her hands through her tangled mane of silver hair. "I had other friends, too, of course—the strongman, the girl who flew on the trapeze—but Maura and I had a special bond."

"Tell us again about your act," Ellie asked, scooting closer.

David rolled his eyes. Grandma Lissa's mouth crooked with a smile, and she leaned in.

"Patrick was the man who could lift cars. Maura was the bearded lady. And I," she said, her eyes lighting, "was the woman who could split from her own shadow."

"Here we go again," David muttered, pulling a video game from his pocket and firing up a match behind his twin sister's back.

"I was the witch," Grandma Lissa said, her hands flying up as she spoke. "I scared them. I made their shadows dance. And for my final act," she spread her arms wide and tilted her head to the sky, "I let my shadow free."

"And then the lions and hippos stood up and sang a cabaret alongside the man in the moon." David got to his feet. "Ellie, come on, we told Mom and Dad we'd check in before dinner."

"Fine," Ellie grumbled. She turned to Grandma Lissa.

"After we eat, I want to hear about the animals."

"Come on." David grabbed his sister's arm. They were too old for all that make-believe circus crap. His father had told them the truth years ago—how Grandma Lissa had run away when she was a teenager, and that she'd convinced herself she had been in the circus as a coping mechanism.

"David," Ellie hissed the second they were out of their grandmother's earshot. "That was rude."

"So is lying to us," he countered. "You know as well as I do that she was never in the circus."

"At least I'm polite about it!" Ellie retorted. "I pretend to believe. You know what Mom said. You know that she's sick. I'm sure it doesn't make her feel better that her grandson accuses her of lying to her face."

David felt a pang in his stomach. "You're right. I'm sorry," he said.

Ellie crossed her arms. "And you can bet that Mom and Dad wouldn't be too happy if they heard that you harassed your dying grandmother."

David let out a groan. Ellie was insufferable sometimes. "What's it going to take?"

"My attic cleaning shift," she replied, a smile settling across her face.

"Oh, come on! That's not fair!" he protested. "That's way too much! All I did was ignore her a little bit!"

"That's not what Mom's going to hear," Ellie said, tilting her head. She pouted. "She'll ground you for a month when she hears you cussed Grandma Lissa out."

David threw his hands up in the air. "You're horrible."

"So we have a deal?"

"Kids! How's Lisbet doing?" his mom asked, wiping her hands on her apron. "Does she need any help on the stairs

Secret Keepers 91

coming down for dinner?"

Ellie shot David a look. He did a quick skim of his options. He could try to tell Mom what had happened first, to make Ellie look like a liar, but Mom trusted Ellie more than she trusted him. He could do nothing, and let Ellie tell her that he swore at his grandmother, and deal with the consequences for that, or he could take the goddamn attic chore time.

"Deal," David grumbled. His mom frowned.

"Deal for what? What deal?"

"Deal... deal that I'll help Grandma Lissa downstairs for dinner as long as you serve ice cream with the pie tonight," David lied through his teeth.

His mother nodded. "Sure. Els, can you come help me in the kitchen?"

"Of course, Mom," Ellie said. She turned and stuck her tongue out at David as she entered the kitchen. He flipped her off. "Mom!" Ellie said, and David's heart skipped a beat.

"What, honey?" his mom asked.

Ellie gave David a sickly sweet smile. "Can we have the French vanilla?"

"Sure," his mother said, bewildered. "David, go help Lisbet."

David glared at Ellie. "Of course," he said, teeth clenched.

* * *

"I know you don't believe me," Grandma Lissa said as she made her way out of bed.

David froze. "What do you mean?"

"I know you think I'm crazy," she said, reaching for her cane. It had an elephant carved along the stem. "That's okay."

"I don't think you're crazy," David said, biting his tongue.

He really should have been more careful what he said around her—Ellie had a point. She was old, and sick, and he should try to be nicer to her.

His grandmother smiled. "Yes, you do."

What was he supposed to say? *No, Grandma Lissa, I completely believe that you ran away and joined the circus, and that your best friend was a bearded lady, and that you can control the shadows.* Shadow controlling wasn't even a real circus act! Her brain couldn't even bother to come up with a real act!

"Mom made pie for dessert," he said, following her over to the staircase, "with French vanilla ice cream."

"Delightful," his grandmother said. "Could you help me here?"

"Yeah," David said, slipping his arm around her waist to stabilize her. "I got you."

They made their way down the stairs, him supporting her. He could feel her ribs beneath her nightgown, and every vein on her exposed skin popped like they were water-colored onto her body.

"Thank you," Grandma Lissa said when they reached the bottom of the stairs. David let go. "Which of you is taking a turn cleaning the attic tomorrow?"

David cleared his throat. "I am, Grandma."

"I thought it was Ellie," she said, walking forward. He noticed the shadow she cast along the hardwood floor of the room. The way the light hit her made her cane look almost like a third leg.

"Me, too," David said.

* * *

The pull-down ladder let out a grinding creak as it yawned down from the ceiling trapdoor. David coughed, waving the dust away, and wrenched it the rest of the way to the ground. He was so going to get Ellie back for this.

The stairs were sketchy at best. Each step groaned with his weight as he ascended. He said a silent thanks when he reached the top in one piece.

David flicked on his flashlight and set the garbage bags he'd brought with him on the floor. The attic wasn't very large in terms of square footage, but the leaning piles of junk crammed into every corner turned small into claustrophobic.

Dark beams of wood stretched across the ceiling at seemingly random intervals and David had to keep his head bowed to avoid smacking into them. Light streamed from the square cut in the floor of the attic, fading out after a few feet so the corners of the attic were still draped in shadow and cobweb. He had to watch his step as he moved through the space. Lone nails and uneven boards stuck up wherever they pleased.

There was supposedly a chain to turn on the light hanging somewhere from the ceiling. He felt around for a while, then found it and tugged. Nothing.

"Great," David muttered, giving the string another yank. "Just great."

The instructions from his parents were pretty clear. Anything that seemed like it might be valuable, or that might have sentimental value to Grandma Lissa, would be kept up in the attic. Everything else would be trashed. David thought it was morbid—they were essentially starting the postmortem cleaning while she was still living in the house. But he didn't have any other choice, and so he picked a corner at random and sat down.

Most of what was in the attic turned out to be utter garbage. Soggy cardboard boxes. Old fabrics laden with mothballs. A gumball machine with a spider web crack stretching the height of the glass, still half-filled with little colorful spheres. David pocketed one before he bagged the machine. Maybe he'd give it to Ellie as payback.

He reached a little wooden box with a rusty lock. It was probably trash, but his parents would want him to check and make sure it didn't have jewelry inside. David brushed the lock and it crumbled off in his hand.

The box opened to reveal letters, penned in large looping cursive on yellowed paper. He pulled one out and shone the flashlight over its surface, trying to make out the words. Almost everything was indecipherable, and some of the words looked like they weren't even in English. He scanned down to the signature at the bottom of the page: *Maura Kofflor.*

His grandmother's voice echoed through his mind. Maura was the bearded lady. He shook his head. She had to know more than one Maura. It was just a coincidence. And even if it wasn't a coincidence, the doctor had said that she might weave details from her life into her story, in order to convince herself it was real. It could be the two Mauras were the same woman, but not a bearded one, and certainly not one in a circus.

David tucked the letterbox to the side and continued with his cleaning.

* * *

"Els," David whispered that night, turning over to face her. They lay on the living room floor, camped out in sleeping bags.

"What?" Ellie asked. "Bad dream? You want me to turn on the lights?"

"No," David said. He turned the words over in his mouth. "Do you ever wonder if Grandma Lissa is telling the truth?"

"What?" Ellie asked again, propping herself up on her elbows. "What do you mean?"

"About being in the circus."

Ellie shook her head. "The doctor said she manufactured the memories, David. It didn't happen."

"But she ran away," he said. "How do they know where she was and wasn't?"

"They know horrible things happened to her," Ellie said, her voice quiet. "They know where she was eventually found. Dad saw her struggle while he grew up. He thinks we should just be happy that she has a fantasy now."

David was quiet for a minute. "But what if," he paused. "What if she's telling the truth? I mean, not about the shadows or anything, but about the circus? Or at least about some of the people?"

"David, that's crazy," Ellie said. "Being around her this much is wigging you out. Don't worry, Mom said we're leaving tomorrow before lunchtime."

"But—"

"Just try to get some sleep, okay?" Ellie said, snuggling back into her sleeping bag. "Good night."

"'Night," he replied, but his words felt hollow.

* * *

The next morning, he was at work in the attic again right after breakfast. Ellie was helping Grandma Lissa sort through the bags he'd already brought down. They were set to leave at noon, and he was supposed to sort through the junk right up until they left.

David went through the boxes slower than he had the day before, keeping an eye out for anything like the letter box, anything that could tell him more about his grandmother's past. Maybe if he could find some more letters, or a picture, he could weave together a better picture of Grandma Lissa's life.

Even when looking carefully and sorting in a more lenient manner, ninety percent of the stuff in the attic was trash. He found a stretch of weathered fabric along the back wall that he tucked aside, but other than that, the boxes contained mostly clothing and rotting garbage.

The musky beam from his flashlight traveled across the attic as he searched and cleaned. David thought back to the conversation with his sister from the night before. *The doctor said she manufactured the memories. They know horrible things happened to her. We should just be happy that she has a fantasy now.*

He knew it was the truth, and he knew he should believe it. The name Maura on the letter was a coincidence. And his grandmother's health and mental state had been faltering since before he was born.

Still, that one question bothered him. *What if?*

"David, wheels up in five minutes!" his dad called up through the open trapdoor. "Make sure you bring the new bags down!"

Something gleamed red under the light from his flashlight. David took a step closer. It was a wooden chest, tucked into the very back corner of the room. His brow furrowed and he strode over. How had he missed that before?

The lock on the chest was much stronger than that of the letter box and it took a few hits from his hammer to crack it open.

His hands drifted over the rough wood of the lid. Chips of red paint floated down at his touch. He slid his fingers under the top and pushed the lid open.

The very first thing on top was a flyer, striped, with

block-letter text splayed across the top: *Witch of Warrensville*. Beneath the text, there was a picture of a woman in black and white, her shoulders and hair wreathed with dark smudges.

David's hands shook as he removed the flyer from the chest. Beneath it rested ticket stubs, peanut shells, even a few crumpled dollar bills. Below those, he could see a costume, just like the one the woman wore in the picture.

What if?

He held the poster out in front of him, focusing the flashlight on the performer's face. He'd never seen a picture of his grandmother when she was young, but when he unfocused his eyes, the resemblance was there.

"David, time to go!" his mother shouted from below. "Bring the bags down!"

"Two minutes!" David shouted back.

"Now!" she barked. "We're running late!"

He looked desperately to the pile of evidence in the trunk. David brought the flyer to his chest and grabbed as much of the rest as he could, peanut shells and ticket stubs, everything he could hold. He whirled around toward the staircase, racing down—

Crack! The first stair splintered under his weight and he slammed into the ground.

"David!" his mother cried, rushing to his side. "Are you all right? I knew that ladder wasn't solid…"

"I'm fine," he managed, pushing himself to his knees. The poster was gone. Everything from his hands was gone.

He glanced up and saw just the corner of the flyer over the trapdoor square in the ceiling. "I need—up there—"

"We have to go," his mother said, helping him to his feet. "We'll get the bags next time. And we'll bring a real ladder." Before he could say anything, she pulled down on the spring release and the pull-down ladder shot back up into the ceiling, folding like a broken accordion.

"But—" David tried, and his mother steered him toward the car. "Mom, in the attic—I—I found a chest, with—"

"That's nice, honey. We'll check it out next visit. Come on, Ellie!" she shouted into the house, shepherding David out the front door. His sister sprinted out the door and toward the car.

"Ellie, wait—last night I found something—" David started.

"Get in the car, dork! We have to go!" Ellie hissed. "Mom's mad because Dad did email instead of cleaning the kitchen, and Grandma Lissa only got through like three boxes. The last thing we want to do is push it right now."

"But," David tried, and Ellie pulled him into the car, shutting the door behind him. "Els, I found something in the attic, a poster of Grandma—"

"Time to go!" his mother slid into the front seat and started the car. "Mark! Come on!"

His dad slipped into the passenger seat, hefting a backpack in after him. "Sorry, guys," he made a face at the backseat. "I know how much you like spending time with your grandmother. But we'll be back soon."

"It's fine," Ellie said before David could say anything. "We're all good back here."

David opened his mouth to say something, but the car's tires squealed on the driveway. He turned back, looking to the house. Grandma Lissa stepped out onto the porch, the wind whipping her hair into a silver frenzy around her face. As they pulled away, David swore he saw a dark form rise next to her. Grandma Lissa started back toward the door. The figure stayed. As David watched, it waved, then turned and entered the house alongside his grandmother.

www.ingramcontent.com/pod-product-compliance
Lightning Source LLC
LaVergne TN
LVHW040156080526
838202LV00042B/3182